EMBRACE YOUR CALLING
AS A CHRISTIAN
WOMAN AT WORK

A COLLABORATIVE RESOURCE BY IWORK4HIM

JIM & MARTHA BRANGENBERG

HIGH BRIDGE BOOKS
HOUSTON

God has given each of you a gift from his great variety of spiritual gifts. Use them well to serve one another.

—1 Peter 4:10 NLT

Work willingly at whatever you do, as though you were working for the Lord rather than for people.

—Colossians 3:23 NLT

Contents

Introduction

I AM SO EXCITED FOR you to read *sheWorks4Him: Embrace Your Calling as a Christian Woman at Work*. Each chapter has been written by a Christian working woman who has been our guest on the *iWork4Him* show. We have heard their hearts on the air and asked them to share their unique work experiences in this book. Each chapter also includes thought-provoking, spiritually challenging questions designed to help you shape your perspective as a Christian working woman. These can work in a small group of trusted friends or just with you and the Lord all alone.

Why did we do this project? Because as a Christian working woman, you need to know you are not the only one struggling to live out your purpose in your work. We learn a lot from other people's faith stories, so it is our hope and prayer that each chapter helps you feel more celebrated, validated, understood, and resourced for living out your faith in your work.

I have never met a woman who wasn't working hard, trying to be everything to everyone. Your workplace may be at home or in a high-rise; almost all women suffer from trying to do it all. TJ Tison describes this complex in her book, *Killing Wonder Women* (TJ wrote a chapter in *iWork4Him: Change the Way You Think About Your Faith at Work*). We want you to embrace who God created you to be, not fulfill the expectations of culture or the church.

God has given you a unique set of gifts, talents, and abilities. Your spiritual gifts are from Him. First Peter 4:10 NLT says, "God has given each of you a gift from his great variety of spiritual gifts. Use them well to serve one another." He gifted you to do the things you are doing. He placed you in the workplace you are in because He needed and wanted you there. You were called into the world to be a living and breathing example of the Gospel in your work. As you turn each page, you will see how God has led these Christian working women to serve in their job more effectively, using their unique giftedness.

Sisters, you are a gift and a blessing. With your busy schedule, it's easy to let your priorities suffer. Remember this. Your number one priority is growing in your life with Christ, getting closer to the Father every day. All other priorities seem to fall in order when we keep Him as our number one.

The amazing women who wrote each chapter are willingly sharing a part of their story to both encourage and challenge you. I pray that it will launch you with renewed purpose in your workplace mission field.

—**Jim Brangenberg**, Talk Show Host and Mentor, www.iWork4Him.com

iWork4Him Media recognizes the value and needs of Christian working women. Over the years, we have conducted many talk show interviews focused on women like you. Each contributor in this book has an interview show link at the end of their chapter. We hope you will listen to these interviews to get to know the authors even better. Below is a small sampling of other sheWorks4Him shows.

sheWorks4Him Show samples

- http://bit.ly/38kVRBc
- http://bit.ly/38ot1Qz
- http://bit.ly/3hVXqc6
- http://bit.ly/399ubOQ
- www.iWork4Him.com/sheworks4him

1

What Hat Do I Wear Today?

Martha Brangenberg

AS A LITTLE GIRL, I HAD an extensive hat collection. I'm pretty sure it started because someone told me I looked good in a hat. The red sunbonnet made from bandana material made me feel sweet and old-fashioned. I loved wearing the patchworked, floppy sunhat to shade my face when relaxing outside. I splurged on a black felt Fedora to wear to the 8th-grade disco dance. My hat collection's crowning jewel had to be the coveted maroon and gold sombrero worn only as a costume and clumsy to display! The hat tree in my bedroom held dozens of options, *but I could only wear one at a time*, and the one selected depended on my activities.

Hats can symbolize a specific time in history, a fashion statement, a culture, or a purpose. No matter which hat is on my head, I am still the same person underneath. *I may look different based on which hat I am wearing, but I am still 100% the same person.*

The same is true of our lives—we wear many symbolic hats. I may be making lunches, posting journal entries, merchandising a store, teaching a small group Bible study, or hosting an interview, but it's all the same person doing these things! *God has given me many different roles to fill but one life to live.* It would be exhausting to change hats all day long.

So, I ask myself these questions:

- What hat represents my role as a Jesus-follower?

- Would I take it off before I put another one on?

- Would I put another hat on top of my "faith hat" and hide it?

- Should my faith hat be a part of my daily wardrobe, no matter what job I am doing?

Second Corinthians 5:17 says, "When someone becomes a Christian, he becomes a brand-new person inside. He is not the same anymore. A new life has begun!" (TLB). If this is true for me, and Jesus changes me, then I have a permanent hat to wear, and according to the Bible, it's a *crown* (2 Tim. 4:8). I can wear this crown everywhere I go and for everything I do. *This crown is integrated into my wardrobe and sets the environment for **all** that I do.* Just think, no more hat changes, and we get to wear a tiara every day.

> *Just start the day with the crown and leave it on all day.*

In life, women change roles like I used to change hats—often! We may have so many parts we don't even know which hat we are wearing. It can be confusing and tiring to keep changing hats. There is a better way to handle this.

According to Psalms 139:13, He knit us together in our mother's womb. I am not separate pieces but entirely knit together. Ephesians 2:10 says, "For we are God's master-

piece. He has created us anew in Christ Jesus, so we can do the good things he planned for us long ago" (NLT). Our Creator wants to be involved in every detail of our lives, not segmented pieces but *every* part. When I asked Jesus to be my Lord and Savior, He didn't save me just for Sunday morning. Jesus changed me completely, all of me, every minute of every day and every detail of my life. This is good news.

I can do everything wearing the same hat. Just start the day with the crown and leave it on all day. This crown is to be worn everywhere I go and for everything I do. It is integrated into my being and sets the environment for all that I encounter. I'll wear my crown on a Zoom call, in the grocery store, in traffic, taking out the trash, when I post on social media, answering emails, and everywhere in between. It's time to integrate Jesus into every aspect of life as a Christian working woman.

I'll straighten your crown if you straighten mine.

sheWorks4Him will help us see how to wear the crown all day every day. God is giving us a front-row seat to learn from the lives of over a dozen wonderful Christian working women. Some days our crown might be crooked or need to be polished, but that is why we need each other. I'll straighten your crown if you straighten mine.

My view of hats has changed over the years, and I currently only have one hat in my closet: a casual baseball cap that I wear on occasion. I think it's time to trade it in and get a tiara!

Martha Brangenberg
www.iWork4Him.com

Co-host of the *iWork4Him* show, a non-profit ministry serving others by transforming the workplace of every Christian into a mission field.

Born into an entrepreneurial family, Martha is an experienced professional with a demonstrated history of working in insurance, Christian retail, and the broadcast media industries. She is skilled in operations and management and has strong attention to detail and a love of people. Her hobbies include gardening, DIY projects, and mentoring marriages with her husband, Jim.

Books

- *iWork4Him*
- *iRetire4Him*

LinkedIn

- www.linkedin.com/in/martha-brangenberg-iWork4Him/

iWork4Him Show

- http://bit.ly/3bicnnj

Chapter 1 Questions

1. List some of the hats you wear every week.

2. Which hat do you wear the most?

3. Which hat is the most uncomfortable?

4. Which hat do you love to wear most often?

5. As a daughter of the King, your tiara is *the* hat you should be wearing every day. What is keeping you from doing that?

6. Look up Romans 12:2. What kind of mind shift do you need to experience to wear that tiara proudly everywhere you go?

7. In your own words, what does it mean to wear the tiara that Martha talks about?

8. How will this view of the tiara impact your work?

2

Christian Working Women

Caroline Mendez

MY DISCOMFORT AS A Christian working woman started back in 2006 after I (a proud feminist, new age queen, and corporate businesswoman) was born again in a Reformed Church pew in Atlanta, Georgia, on Easter morning.

I spent the next several years learning more about Christ, and growing in my relationship with Him, as I stopped working professionally and served whoever He asked me to. I did every Bible study our church and community offered: how to be a good wife; a faithful, shepherding mother; and a Proverbs 31 woman. But it did not speak to all of me. And the part that consistently was not spoken to was the professional side of me. The Christian professional working woman's side (which was, up until I was born again, a major part of who I was).

So, in my curiosity to know what I was supposed to do with this part of me that was just "dangling there," the search began. The search began on the internet Googling Christian businesswomen and Christian women business groups. My query returned mostly sites about Beth Moore and Joyce Meyer, two women who teach from the Bible, not professional businesswomen.

In the spring of 2010, it was during prayer time that I asked (actually *begged*) for God to give me work (not serving at church or making meals for new moms) that would use my passion for working women and my new identity in Christ. In answer was the message "feed my daughters." The picture that accompanied the message was a beautiful banquet table, full of bountiful food, where businesswomen were joyfully gathered. It had the feel of a Christ-filled executive meeting but with joy and transparency. From 2011 to 2015, I and fellow businesswomen built groups of Christian businesswomen. Our purpose was to provide a community to women who wanted to integrate their faith and work, share their business experience, learn from one another, and grow as godly business leaders.

As these women met together, their stories began to unfold as they deepened their relationships. *They shared common issues of isolation, struggle, disappointment, roadblocks, challenges, and mistakes.*

As the months went by, and they continued to share parts of their stories, you could almost hear deep sighs being released from the depths of their souls. They were realizing, as they listened to each other, they were *not* alone. There were other women in the marketplace, leading and building teams, businesses, non-profits, schools, and serving in governments of every shape and size. And they were not alone. And *they no longer had to "go it alone."*

What was learned from this time of gathering working women in community?

- Many of us *are specifically called to work in the marketplace.* God appoints many women to key positions in the marketplace. Just like Lydia, the seller of purple in the Bible, women today can honor God as believers and as professionals whether we work part-time, full-time, or volunteer for a season or a lifetime.

- Many of us are where we are "for such a time as this." It is not an accident, selfishness, punishment, good fortune, or luck. *God placed each of us in our current organizations, right now, for His highest and best purposes (if* you have sought His counsel about it).

- You need to know that God designed you with a unique mix of gifts, talents, and skills. *He intends for you to use your abilities actively* and not downplay, suppress, question, ignore, or hide them.

- Women are **co-heirs** *with men* in the Kingdom. We are stewards of the flourishing and co-laborers in the cultural mandate, with men. (*The cultural mandate is found in Genesis 1:28, in which God, after having created the world and all in it, ascribes to humankind the tasks of filling, subduing,* **and ruling** *over the earth. The cultural mandate includes the sentence "Be fruitful and multiply"[NLT].)*

- Just because you have never heard a sermon from the pulpit on the many women in the

Bible who contributed to the start of the church, the funding of the church, the building of the church, the leading of Israel, and the development of Christianity around the world, does not mean women were not there. They *were* there and active in planting and leading the church. Pheobe, Junia, Priscilla, and Mary Magdalene are only a few of the women who served in various "church roles" alongside the men. And by the way, not only was Mary Magdalene *not* a prostitute (there is no biblical evidence of it) there by Jesus's side the entire ministry, she, along with a group of women, *funded* his ministry. She was the Apostle to the Apostles. Without Mary, there would be no New Testament.

- And we are doing all these things today, too. We are: *Worthy. Gifted. Relevant. And equally created and gifted and loved and valued in the eyes of God. "So, God created man in his own image, in the image of God he created him; male **and female he created them**."* (Gen. 1:27 ESV)

My experience in the marketplace as a Christian working woman over the past 14 years has been, at times, *shocking due to the state (or lack thereof) of flourishing of my fellow sisters in Christ who work* and the lack of support for them and their calling. From their church, their home, their workplace, and fellow women in their lives. Perhaps, like me, you have been seeing and feeling the same things:

- *Christian women* are rarely affirmed in their spiritual gifts, as well as their natural gifts, talents, and abilities.

- *Christian working women* are rarely affirmed in their work or calling.

- *Christian working women* are rarely mentored by other Christian working women.

- *Christian working women* have few options for community, and what they do have is limited and does not fit the landscape of their life.

- *Christian working women* struggle to engage with other Christian working women because their schedules are full.

- Organizations focused on discipleship for Christian working women are too few, are under-funded and under-resourced.

These are the areas of our lives as working Christ-following women we need to reclaim and prioritize.

Thankfully, now more organizations and churches are waking up to the state of the Christian working woman. There are now Bible studies, groups, professional associations, visible Christian women marketplace leaders, and many others of us, who share a heart for the current plight of Christian working

Let us step into our rightful place in the Kingdom and support and encourage each other "for such a time as this."

women. Women today, more than ever, are finding their voices and living their calling. Praise God! There are now books written by Christian working women *for* Christian working women.

In 2015, the Lord prompted me to search out and interview ten Christian women leaders in the marketplace. The stories of their journeys to leadership and their advice to the next generation of fellow women leaders produced something I was not prepared for. A model. A model of a *Christian **woman** leader* that is defined in the book the Lord led me to write: *Threads of Wisdom: Real World Journeys to Leadership of Christian Women Marketplace Leaders and Their Best Advice for Glorifying God in Your Calling.*

This newly revealed model paints a fresh picture of a true Christian woman working and leading as a daughter of Christ. *As Christian working women and leaders of women, let us step into our rightful place in the Kingdom and support and encourage each other "for such a time as this."*

Caroline A. Mendez
Founder of called4, LLC.

Caroline is a Certified Professional Coach and Facilitator, and catalyst for Christian professional women, leaders, and their organizations. Her passion is to ignite a movement that restores Christian women to their rightful place in the Kingdom and to equip and empower the next generation of Christian women leaders with the legacy wisdom found in her book, *Threads of Wisdom,* and her current role of developing peer forums for Christian women leaders and influencers at Pinnacle Forum.

Book

- *Threads of Wisdom*

LinkedIn

- www.linkedin.com/in/threadwisdom/

iWork4Him Show

- http://bit.ly/3s5SuWr

Chapter 2 Questions

1. As a Christian working woman, what's your most frequent struggle? Is it isolation, disappointment, making mistakes, or roadblocks erected by others?

2. What has changed since you realized you have a call on your life?

3. If you've been judged by people in your church for being a working woman, how have you handled that?

4. We are co-heirs with men to rule the earth. How does that change your work perspective?

5. God made you uniquely a woman and gave you work. What unique assets do you bring to the table as a woman?

6. What did you really hear Caroline say?

7. How will this chapter and these questions impact your work moving forward?

3

Success at Home and Work

Marcia Malzahn

IT WAS A WINTER MORNING in Minnesota, and I rushed to catch the bus to work going downtown Minneapolis. My husband drove me to the bus stop, and because we were running late, he simply yelled, "run!" And I did. There was only one problem: I was nine months pregnant with our second child. When I stepped into the bus, everyone looked at me and I could read their minds thinking, "Oh no, please don't have your child here on this bus!" Don't worry. I didn't. Our son was born a few days later.

You see, I have been a Christian full-time working mother all my life. I married young and had my two children in the first few years of our marriage. I knew that two children were all I could handle working full-time as a community banker. I started as a teller at twenty years old. My career flourished from there, and I made it to Executive Vice President, Chief Financial Officer, and Chief Operating Officer of a community bank I co-founded.

I only have two regrets in my life: 1) I only took six weeks with my baby girl when she was born, and 2) I only took eight weeks with my baby boy when he was born. Due to the lack of available paid time off, I couldn't take more time. And *I could never take that time back with my babies.* Ever since, I have been encouraging women to *take enough time off with their babies so they can cherish those first few months plus get some rest before going back to work.*

As I grew in my career, *I decided to give my children quality time during the few hours I had with them daily.* I also decided to not work on the weekends to have quality family time. During all those years, I prayed daily and asked God to give me grace for each day, so I could work full-time, be a good mom and wife, and handle the household duties.

When my kids were ten and eight years old, I was already a branch manager working fifty hours a week plus driving two hours daily. I then decided to leave my banking career and worked for a church for five years, mainly to spend more time with my family, until I returned to banking to start a community bank.

During those years, I realized *I had attained career success and some level of balance in my life.* A passion emerged within me to share with other women how I had accomplished both. It was February, another winter day, when I told my husband, "I want to help other women be successful in their careers *while* being a successful mom and wife, too." After a long conversation, my husband said, "Why don't you write a devotional?" And so, my journey of writing began with my first book, *Devotions for Working Women: A Daily Inspiration to Live a Successful and Balanced Life.* Let me share something from this book:

As a working woman, you encounter many challenges in balancing life every day. This inspirational book will motivate, encourage, and inspire you to be successful and balanced in every area of your life. It will give you practical examples and tips on living in a way that positively impacts those around you. This book will demonstrate how simple your life can be when you follow basic principles from the Master of balance, our loving God the Father. It will also inspire you to never give up, knowing you are not alone. You have God and the people He has put in your life to help accomplish what He's called you to do. This devotional covers several traits that define a true leader, regardless of your job title:

- *Character* is the most important thing others see in you.

- The Word of God gives you the *encouragement* you need daily to be a woman of integrity.

- *Obedience* to His Word and your trust in Him provides you with the gift of *wisdom*.

- When He sees your *faithfulness* to His teachings, you allow Him to bless you beyond your wildest dreams.

- When you strive to live a life of *holiness*, God can use you to influence other people.

- When you have *thankfulness* in your heart and acknowledge Him in all you have and are, He shows you His amazing love for you.

- It is only by *faith* through grace that you receive the gift of salvation; you cannot earn it by your own deeds.

- *Success* comes when you love God above all things and love others with His love.

- *Balance* is a gift from God that you can obtain by asking Him to help you achieve it daily, and by following His ways.

- True *leadership* is comprised of all the traits above.

Ten years after I started the community bank, I decided to pursue my calling to *help working people be successful in every area of their lives.* I founded Malzahn Strategic, a consulting firm working with community financial institutions, pursued my professional speaking career, founded Crowning Achievements International, and continued to write books. My second book, *The Fire Within: Connect Your Gifts with Your Calling*, is a practical guide to help you find your calling. Because I love friends, I wrote a short book of poems called *The Friendship Book: Because You Matter to Me*. And I just published my fourth book, *Bring YOUR Shoes: A Fresh Perspective for Leaders with Big Shoes to Fill*, to help emerging leaders be successful.

Success comes when you love God above all things and love others with His love.

You're not alone. I encourage you to find your calling, reach out to other Christian working women, and help others along the way. As I write this chapter, I've been married now for thirty-two years, and I'm enjoying every minute with my new baby grandson. God is always faithful!

Marci Malzahn

www.marciamalzahn.com

Marcia "Marci" Malzahn, a native of Nicaragua, came to Minnesota in 1986 and started a career in banking. She co-founded a community bank in Minnesota and is currently president and co-owner of Malzahn Companies and its subsidiaries, Malzahn Strategic, Malzahn Publishing, and Crowning Achievements International. Marci is an international bilingual inspirational speaker, frequently speaking at banking conferences and associations and leadership and women's conferences.

Books

- *Devotions for Working Women*
- *The Fire Within*
- *The Friendship Book* (also in Spanish – *El Libro de la Amistad*)
- *Bring YOUR Shoes*

LinkedIn

- www.linkedin.com/in/marcia-marci-malzahn-7290061/

iWork4Him Show

- http://bit.ly/2Lwlwhr

Chapter 3 Questions

1. As a Christian working woman, you may have some regrets, too. How have you dealt with those regrets? Bring them to the Lord, and He will give you peace.

2. Integrating your work and home life and balancing your attention between the two can be challenging. In what areas do you feel you need help?

3. How are you reaching out to others to help you?

4. In what ways could you set aside a special time for your family?

5. What does success in the workplace and the home mean to you?

6. If you are married, do you and your spouse have a plan to manage work/life challenges? Why/why not?

7. If you are single, who could help you prioritize commitments to spend time with your loved ones and with God?

8. Marcia lists several traits that define true leaders. What traits have you developed, and which ones can you improve?

4

Identity: Why I Burned It

Danita Bye

I'M STANDING IN FRONT OF my closet, contemplating my perfectly arranged corporate navy-blue suits. Which one offers the best protection for the day? Each suit serves its own purpose—the First Call Suit, the Presentation Suit, the Closing Suit.

As I reach for the First Call Suit, I hear a soft whisper in my heart. I've come to recognize this whisper as the voice of the Holy Spirit. I hear, "Danita, I'm the only one who can protect your heart."

My eyes instantly well with tears. I know exactly what this message is about. I'm donning these beautifully tailored suits as if they are my armor, protecting me and my heart from the harshness of the corporate world. I'm desperately hoping that my clients, colleagues, and employees won't see past my I-got-my-act-together image. I don't want them to know that my internal world is chaotic and stressful.

Once again, the nagging question races through my mind: "How can I excel at my high-pressure corporate career ... while being a great wife to Gordon ... and the best mom to three young children?" The questions don't stop there—they keep going. "And, how can I also be a good friend, daughter, church worker, and soccer coach ... all at the same time?"

My tears blur the image of the navy-blue suits. I realize I'm exhausted. There are too many voices telling me who to be and what to do. My external critics blame me for not performing and meeting my goals at work. According to the accusations of my internal critics, I am a failure at home. It's overwhelming.

Between my sobs, I whisper, "God, I want to change. I want to know you, to discover who I am in you, and what you are calling me to do. I want to be real and authentic with you, myself, and others."

This is a life-shifting decision. I've been prioritizing the voices of my critics for most of my life. Now, how do I signal to both my internal and external critics that I'm not going to listen to them anymore? Instead, I'm choosing to prioritize who God says I am and what He is calling me to do.

To mark the gravity of my decision, I decide to burn, to sacrifice, one of my prized navy-blue suits.

Gingerly, I place the suit into the fireplace. I light the fire and watch. The fabric begins to bubble and gurgle as the red-orange flames work to destroy my once beautiful tailored suit. It's as if the fabric is resisting. It looks grotesque. And the smell is putrid, sickening. Then, I hear the Holy Spirit whisper deep inside my heart,

"Danita, that's what your armor is to me—grotesque and sickening."

The sobs become deeper as I confess my life-long habit of looking to others for approval versus looking to God.

Eventually, my tears turn to joy, as I realize that I have been liberated from both the external and internal critics. I dance throughout my house, opening the windows to let the fresh, sweet morning air clean out the stench. I feel happy and free. It's then that I hear the whispering voice again. "The most impactful Danita is the real Danita. Let me be the one to protect you as you show your heart to the world."

I am a woman made in God's image. I am being strategically sent to particular people, places, and nations to accomplish God's purposes and plans.

How did this experience change me? First, I don't wear as many navy-blue suits—I try to dress more creatively. However, even when I do, I don the suit as the authentic Danita, who's okay confessing when she is confused or hurt. When I mess up, whether at home or work, I recognize that God is my protector. I can trust Him.

Three Steps to Live Authentically

Staying focused on my relationship with my Heavenly Father and my God's plans for my life versus what I think others expect of me and how I condemn myself is a daily journey for me. To help me stay focused, I use the Inward,

Outward, Upward model. I invite you to consider integrating some of these ideas into your life.

1. Focus Inward

My internal thinking patterns can do more damage than any criticism from the outside. Here are some ways that I stay attuned to the guidance of the Holy Spirit versus listening to my internal critics.

- *Redefine Success Messaging.* We are constantly bombarded by marketing messages, selling an impossible model of what success looks like. To counteract this trend, I have a morning ritual. I repeat the words that I have written on a business card shortly after my navy-blue-suit bonfire: *I am exactly who I am supposed to be.* I am a woman made in God's image. I am being strategically sent to particular people, places, and nations to accomplish God's purposes and plans.

- These words reaffirm two truths. First, they remind me of who I am and my relationship as a daughter to the Heavenly Father. Next, they help me to embrace what I am called to do: to be an ambassador for the Most High King. My husband thinks it's a little weird for me to be talking to myself every morning, but he is getting more accustomed to it.

What is your internal critic telling you that's holding you back from living a fulfilled life?

2. Focus Outward

Believing unfounded criticisms from friends, family, and colleagues impacts my ability to live authentically. Here are some ways that I deal with the lies from external critics:

- *Identify the Lies*. I journal most days. I listen to my self-talk and what I am saying about myself. If the thought is a lie, I make a note in my journal. Sometimes, I'm amazed at the filth that's in my head!

- *Destroy the Lies*. In the next step, I write each lie on a piece of paper. I say them out loud, followed by, "This is a lie." I tear the paper into small pieces. This is a physical reminder that I have broken the lies, and they no longer have control over me.

- *Install the Truth*. When I remove a lie, I want to replace that space with the truth. Otherwise, another lie will take its place, or the old one will come back. In my journal, I put a big "X" through the lie and then write the truth on the opposite side of the page. It's helpful to write the truth statements on flashcards to remind yourself of how God sees the perfect woman He created. When I see some lies that keep seeping into my life, I write them on a card, take them to my fireplace, and have a burning ceremony.

How can you embrace the truth about who God created you to be versus conforming to who you think others want you to be?

3. Focus Upward

By focusing on what God says about me, I learn to embrace my unique skills, talents, and even my vulnerabilities. This gives me the confidence to be authentic as I interact with people. I remind myself that the old navy-blue suit armor did not protect my heart. Only God can do that.

Here are some steps I take to focus upward so that I walk more aligned with God's purposes and plans in my life. I'm confident they will be helpful to you too.

- *Join a Community of Believers.* A "community of believers" is not only the members of *your* church in *your* town but can be family, colleagues, and friends from all over the globe. My fellow believers assist me in identifying and breaking the lies in my life.

- *Claim the Power of Prayer.* Prayer provides the basis for shifting my unhealthy thinking patterns and how I view challenges in my life. Challenges aren't always obstacles. If I wait and watch, I will often see the bigger picture of how God uses challenges in guiding me on my life journey.

- *Meditate on Scripture.* Christian meditation is a powerful tool to learn about your full identity and how God wants to use it for his purposes. Whenever I think of something I would like to meditate on, I write it down on the back of one of my old business cards. I take some of them with me when I'm out on a walk. They're small and practical, and it keeps my mind focused as I'm meditating.

What is holding you back from living the life God had planned for you even before you were born?

As you are standing in front of your closet, what are the "navy-blue suits" that *you* need to "burn?"

What are you holding onto as your perceived protection from the harshness of the world?

If you're exhausted by your constant efforts to shield your vulnerabilities from the world, it's time to take a break. You are fully protected by God's grace. His purpose and plans for your life will be your shield and your true armor.

Danita Bye, M.A.
www.DanitaBye.com

Danita is an executive leadership and sales development expert. She's been a contributing author to the Forbes Coaches Council, sales coach for Harvard Business School MBA students, and a TEDx speaker on Millennial leadership. She's been published in Forbes, Huffington Post, and CEO World.

She is a mother of three millennials, has four grandchildren, and operates her global headquarters from the Cornerstone Ranch in North Dakota.

Book

- *Millennials Matter: Proven Strategies for Building Your Next-Gen Leader*

LinkedIn

- www.linkedin.com/in/danitabye

iWork4Him Shows

- http://bit.ly/35kdoY9
- http://bit.ly/3ougoc8
- http://bit.ly/2L5mz8e

Chapter 4 Questions

1. What are the "navy blue suits" that you need to "burn?" These are the beliefs that are holding you back from living the life God had planned for you.

2. What are you holding onto as an unnecessary part of your identity?

3. How might you stay attuned to the guidance of the Holy Spirit versus listening to your internal critic?

4. How can you differentiate between the truth about who God created you to be versus what you believe others want you to be?

5. How can you deal with your external critics so that you destroy the lies you hear?

6. How will you focus upward so that you can walk in God's purposes and plans for your life?

7. What did you really hear Danita Say?

8. How will this impact your work?

5

Confidence in Christ Matters

Catherine Gates

IT BROKE MY HEART TO hear yet another woman say, "I wish I could figure out how to be more like a man. Then I would be successful." I know many women who feel this way, but it's simply an insidious lie. I had experienced the challenges that influenced women to adopt this belief. And something in my spirit said, "Enough." I was finally compelled to act.

My goal was to help women see the valuable contributions they can make because of how God created them. I organized a panel of two women and two men to discuss the difference it makes when women are encouraged to apply their feminine strengths at work. I got approval for us to present at a women's networking event. We were invited to present that topic at three other organizations that year: two women's events and one for communications professionals including men and women. The responses from women were the same at each event: "Thank you so much for presenting this topic. I have struggled with being a woman in a male-dominated field, and this gave me permission to be myself, along with ideas on how to be more successful being true to who I am."

Three years later, I joined the National Association of Mothers' Centers, a non-profit organization. Our team proactively advocated for more women in leadership in our government and businesses. That's when I became aware of just how significant the deficit of women leaders was and still is in our country.

In 2007, women held only six percent of executive positions in Fortune 500 companies[1]. Today, more than thirteen years later, we are still having the same conversations. When I talk with women across many different industries and at all levels of organizations, the one thing that is striking to me is the fact that very little has changed. And since moving to Arkansas, living in the Bible Belt has made me exceptionally aware of the added pressures and cultural expectations many Christian women encounter.

> Studies have shown that when women have a seat at the table, they help bring about greater success.

The combination of messages from our culture and the church influences us to think women are not as cut out for leadership as men. That our rightful place is in subordinate roles. This is simply an outright lie that we can't afford to buy into. Women can have exceptional leadership skills and abilities that contribute to innovation and

---

[1] Eagly and Carli, "Women and the Labyrinth of Leadership."

competitive differentiation. Studies have shown that when women have a seat at the table, they help bring about greater success.

Companies with women on the board outperform companies with no women on the board by 26%, according to the article on BusinessInsider.com[2] "Companies with Women on the Board Crush Companies That are Only Men" from September 2014.

According to a Morgan Stanley report[3], "more gender diversity, particularly in corporate settings, can translate to increased productivity, greater innovation, better products, better decision-making, and higher employee retention and satisfaction.""

Let's go back to Genesis for a moment.

God created man *and* woman in His image (Genesis 1:27) and gave us both the same cultural mandate: to fill and subdue the earth (Genesis 1:28). Eve was created to be a *strong* support, equal to Adam, blessed with strengths to offer where he was weak.[4] The original phrase in Genesis 2:20 translated "helper fit" (ESV) is *ezer kenegdo*. The word *ezer* is used in other places in the Bible for God, describing Him as Israel's helper, and at times when Israel is appealing to other nations for military help. Eve was taken out of Adam to be an equal partner that would complete him[5].

---

[2] Archer, "Companies with Women in Leadership Roles Crush the Competition."

[3] "An Investor's Guide to Gender Diversity."

[4] "Why Did God Use Adam's Rib to Create Eve?"

[5] "Ezer Kenegdo."

God designed women and men to work together, side by side, so that we can have the best world and lives possible. We are each blessed with different skills and talents. But each of us is of equal value and importance. The Fall caused a serious rift in that design. Still, the stories in both the Old Testament and New Testament show us how God wasted no time setting His redemptive plan in motion. Each step in His plan over thousands of years has required the courage, strength, and talents of both men and women.

Here are just a few examples:

- *Miriam*, the older sister of Moses, was a leader alongside her brothers, Moses and Aaron. She kept Moses safe when he was a baby and spoke up fearlessly against injustices. She led the people in celebration after the Israelites crossed the Red Sea in safety and saw the Egyptians destroyed.

- *Ruth* lost her husband and chose to follow her mother-in-law to Bethlehem, where she was a foreigner. There, she worked in the fields to provide for the two of them. Boaz noticed Ruth and redeemed her, taking her as his wife. Ruth and Boaz are in the lineage of Jesus Christ.

- *Esther* and Mordecai were exiles in Persia. Mordecai was in the king's court and Esther, an orphan, became queen. By her faith and courage, Esther used her influence with the king to save the Jewish people from being destroyed by their enemies.

- *Priscilla* and Aquila worked alongside Paul and risked their lives for Paul and the spreading of the Gospel.

Those women demonstrated bravery, wisdom, and leadership. *The challenges we face today also require the bravery, wisdom, and leadership of both women and men.* But when you look at the corporate landscape across industries today, the numbers are still as low as five percent in some industries, going up to only 20 percent in others[6]. Followers of Christ have an opportunity to lead the way toward change that supports all people in fulfilling their God-given potential.

My study of God's Word has helped me to see that God values all people equally. He has created each of us to do good works that He prepared for us (Ephesians 2:10). Each of us has our part to play as part of a greater whole (Romans 12:4–5). We need to guard against what the world says about us, for better or worse. If you want your identity and confidence to be immovable, unshakable, and empowering, you have to put it in the One who doesn't change—Jesus Christ.

What can we do? Women need to be willing to have the faith to allow the leader inside them to show up in their actions and words. Find healthy ways to speak up when their ideas are dismissed or overlooked for growth

---

[6] Warner, Ellman, and Boesch, "The Women's Leadership Gap."

opportunities. To do that successfully, we need to go deeper in our understanding of the work God has done and continues to do in and through us. We need to have real, transparent conversations with our male leaders to gain their support. And we need to support one another. Our relationship with God must be our absolute top priority. After all, Jesus didn't die for us so we could be angry, defensive, or defeated.

Here are immediate steps women can take to become catalysts for needed change.

- *Clear out the old BS (belief systems) and replace them with Truth.* It's going to take self-awareness and diligence to dig up the lies, the ones that say, "I'm not enough," "I have to have it all figured out," "I have to be something I'm not, to move up." We need to replace those lies with the truth from God's Word. You are a daughter of the King (Rom. 8:16–17). You are more than a conqueror (Rom. 8:37). You are Christ's ambassador (2 Cor. 5:20). When you focus on what God says about you, you will gain the confidence to keep going.

- *Seek God's help through prayer.* Jesus told us in John 16:23–24 that when we ask, we will receive. God is always there for us, ready to provide wisdom, direction, insight, and favor when we ask Him for help. When you're not sure what to do, ask God. Make prayer a priority at all times (Eph. 6:18).

- *Encourage and support other women.* We don't have a God of scarcity. There are abundant opportunities and blessings for those who are faithful. Find community with other women and encourage one another (Heb. 10:24–25). Support each other and watch the difference it makes for everyone.

All of us have a greater opportunity to thrive in a world where men and women work together to complete one another cooperatively, collaboratively, and with complete respect for each other's unique skills and abilities as God designed them. It's time for women to boldly rise up to lead, for men to step up to support and mentor women, and for all of us to courageously participate in changing the conversation.

First Corinthians 11:11 says, "Nevertheless, in the Lord woman is not independent of man nor man of woman" (ESV). Our roles may be different in various situations. *When men and women work together with God at the center, we are strong and complete, in a state of wholeness.* There is peace or Shalom. This isn't a competition. It's time for a transformation. I pray that we maximize the potential of all people, moving toward the unity Christ prayed for us to experience (John 17:12-23). And may it all be for the glory of God and the building of His Kingdom.

Catherine Gates
www.WomeninMarketplace.net

Catherine Gates is Executive Director for Women in the Marketplace, a nonprofit ministry equipping working women to confidently pursue their faith and career for the glory of God. Prior to that, she was Senior Director of Content and Partnerships for Workmatters. Catherine has diverse experience in technology, training, non-profit management, sales coaching and training, public speaking and writing. Catherine is passionate about helping people achieve more of their God-given potential.

Catherine is on the board of Ladies of Grace, a women's prison ministry; on the leadership team for Christian Women in the Workplace; and a member of the Women's Empowerment Center Executive Advisory Council. She is married to Thomas Gates and has one adult son.

Book

- *The Confidence Cornerstone: A Woman's Guide to Fearless Leadership*

LinkedIn

- www.linkedin.com/in/catherinejrgates/

iWork4Him Shows

- http://bit.ly/35nL5Z8
- http://bit.ly/3nqggsX

Chapter 5 Questions

1. What valuable contributions have God created you to provide in your work?

2. What kind of leadership/workplace challenges do you face today? What do you need to do to meet them with bravery and wisdom?

3. What are the lies in your belief system that need to be corrected and removed?

4. Where can you find community with other Christian working women?

5. Provide an example of men and women working together on a problem, with God at the center, bringing strength and completeness into a solution. What were the results?

6. What did you really hear Catherine say?

7. How will this impact your work?

6

True Purpose, One Calling

Angela Sackett

ALL MY LIFE, I HUNTED for what I was "called" to do. From childhood, I excelled in performance. I wrote and performed monologues for local and national organizations, acting in church plays, community theatre, and commercials. I sang with praise teams in youth group and "big church," as we called it, and danced and taught classical ballet in a Christian arts company. Pursuing a theatre and Bible degree in college, I was certain I'd eventually work at a megachurch, leading theatre productions, and probably be married to a youth pastor.

As it happens, I did follow a very similar path. My beloved led a parachurch ministry and became ordained at a church where we sang together and where I wrote and directed dramatic productions. We hosted weekly gatherings in our church and our home, discipling young adults. We were blessed with a quiver-full of children (five, to be exact) along the way and began home-educating. Simultaneously, I started a side business in photography, which eventually allowed us to work together as a couple. There were so many roles to play and plates to spin; I became adept at seemingly holding all the pieces together for any onlookers. I thought I needed to run after all the things I could do well, and I needed to somehow find my "true purpose." These opposing messages caused plenty of internal stress. Having been raised with a high-achieving, feminist single parent placed a lot of pressure on me as a young woman. In addition, my church tradition prioritized positivity and good appearance. I believed at my core that others needed to see I could do it all and do it well.

Proverbs 31, so often referred to in women's studies, can add to this feeling when you read from that worldview. Maybe you have also read about Esther, Deborah, Rahab, or one of "the Marys" or other famous women of the Bible. Possibly you, like me, have heard their stories as a call to greatness. Surely, if these women can rise early, care for their households and run businesses, stand up to evil kings or conquer wicked men on the battlefield, govern communities or walk out of prostitution and into the lineage of Jesus, we can master all the roles in our own lives. *Certainly, we can wife and mother and business-manage well, all the while pursuing our one elusive "purpose," keeping a joyful countenance and a clean floor. Can't we?*

I have come to believe our "purpose" is much simpler than we often make it. I no longer think there's one perfect job we must discover and do for the rest of our lives. It is likely our "jobs" will look different and require varying levels of focus—including the ability to selectively ignore them—in different seasons. Ultimately, there is only one calling we must pursue with all our hearts. *Distraction and* *the tendency to try to do "all the things" may well be the ene-mies of the **core calling** that must infuse our lives and define all our work.*

In another oft-told story about women, Luke 10 notes a seemingly small moment that is, in fact, huge to its char-acters. Martha is hosting a gathering. The Guest of Honor is arguably the most important of all time. This story is often taught as a diatribe against Martha, "the workahol-ic," and by contrast, a lovely portrait of Mary, who did nothing but sit and worship.

Prayerfully, I honor the intention of this passage when I read it, not as a dividing picture of two women. Rather than Martha being the "bad girl," I see distraction fluster-ing her and placing her in danger of being more controlled by her work than being led by her gentle Master. After years of being "worried and bothered and anxious about so many things" myself (Luke 10:41b, Amplified Version), I now see these verses as an invitation: "Don't let the work distract you or make you anxious, little one, but worship while you work and take time to sit at my feet."

There are three things I have come to believe about our work. I pray they encourage you and energize you with joy at our Father's invitation!

1. There is freedom to put our work "on pause" because of Jesus.

Our Lord certainly doesn't call us to stop all work for all time; He does call us to stop regularly to worship Him. Mary was not a better Christian woman because she wasn't helping Martha. She chose what was most needed, according to Jesus, amid plenty of work: a single-minded focus on the One she loved more. Our willingness to temporarily interrupt our work at His leading shows our proper worship for Him and builds our trust in His provision.

2. Our work will be unique, and it may change over seasons.

In Him, no one job is necessarily more important; almost all work can be used to further the Gospel message. Whether it's helping a working neighbor with her kiddos, kindly serving customers, or advising others in Kingdom-minded financial investment, work is for His glory!

When I came as a distressed teen to live with my dad, my stepmom relinquished several church roles to minister to me as her new daughter. Others didn't understand, but the fruit of my mom's sacrifice is still growing today.

Any "calling" I have can be distilled to this one: Love Him and love people with His love.

You may discover you can't devote the time and creative energy you're called to as a mom and still hold a full-time career. You might need to drop ministry responsibilities to care for an ailing family member. You may be called to courageously step into unknown job territory. *There is freedom from God to grow as you go!*

3. Any "calling" I have can be distilled to this one:
Love Him and love people with His love.

There's such freedom here! Our Master *does* call us to do *all* work with our eyes, mind, and heart fully on Him.

Whatever work this season may bring, we can trust that we are about our "one calling" when we walk in His freedom, trust Him to lead us His way, and determine to give Him glory in every job, whether it appears big or small.

> And now, Israel, what does the LORD your God require of you, but to fear the LORD your God, to walk in all his ways, to love him, to serve the LORD your God with all your heart and with all your soul, and to keep the commandments and statutes of the LORD, which I am commanding you today for your good? Behold, to the LORD your God belong heaven and the heaven of heavens, the earth with all that is in it.
> (Deut. 10:12–14 ESV)

Angela Sackett

www.EverydayWelcome.com
www.DancingWithMyFather.net

Angela is a wife, home-educating momma of five (plus a daughter-in-love), and most of all, Jesus girl (and she's terrible at dusting). She's an author, women's event speaker, professional photographer, and professional blogger. Find her at EverydayWelcome.com.

At Everyday Welcome, I share recipes, devotional content, and inspiration for heart and home. I want to help equip you to open your heart and open your home to know the love of Jesus and make Him known to those in your life and at your table.

LinkedIn

- www.linkedin.com/in/angela-sackett-92a06335/

iWork4Him Show

- http://bit.ly/3pRFVMK

Chapter 6 Questions

1. Where did the pressure come for you to be like a Proverbs 31 woman?

2. What task do you know needs to be eliminated from your overwhelmed schedule?

3. What do you think is your true purpose?

4. What distractions do you need to remove right now so you can focus on your true purpose?

5. Think of two ways to find time to pause during your work.

6. How do you process when your work changes but
   your purpose doesn't?

7. What did you really hear Angela say?

8. How will this impact your work?

7

Woman of the World or Woman of the Word

Donna Clute

PROVERBS 31 IS A POWERFUL chapter of wisdom. The woman described in this passage seems unattainable. Yet every day, if we take pause and observe, we can find examples of this heroine. For you, perhaps it was your mom or grandmother, maybe an aunt or close family friend or your pastor's wife. Sometimes this passage can be a burden to a woman, causing her to feel like she has something to prove.

In light of the passage, I have learned that in life, ministry, business, and family, there is no such thing as the Lone Ranger, nor do I need to prove myself. *Nobody really goes it alone for very long,* and trying to live up to an unattainable measure will wear you out.

In Genesis, the Bible tells us woman was created to be man's partner[1] , and there was never a revision in God's Word from the original intention for woman, although, like man, she was created to be in relationship and partnership with the Lord. So as a woman, my *first responsibility is to be in partnership with the Lord[2] to serve in the mission field where He has planted me*. Since I am married (not a requirement if you are single), my second responsibility is to be in partnership with my husband[1]. Because my husband and I have children, my third responsibility is to be in partnership with my children. In business, my responsibility is to be in partnership with my boss/company to serve clients or customers[3]. In life, my responsibility is to be in partnership with friends and other extended family members. In church and ministry, it is my responsibility to partner with other believers to evangelize, disciple, teach, and serve.

It is the sin of pride or the lies of the enemy that lead us on a path of aloneness. On that path are detours to the ideals of the world that distract us away from the truths of the Word. Even though I have been a believer nearly all my life, I fail to always tap into my real source for direction and truth.

Among the lies and areas of pride I struggled with, I believed I had to be tough to dominate in business, or that I had to be all things to all people so as not to let anyone

---

[1] Genesis 2:18, Genesis 2:24

[2] Exodus 20:3, Deuteronomy 5:7, Romans 8:17

[3] 1 Peter 2:18, Colossians 2:23–24

down. I wore myself out and hurt relationships. I dishonored God and discredited the validity of the Christian faith. *In all of it, my heart was to be a good businessperson, a good wife and mom, and a valuable friend, yet I crashed and failed.*

In short, like many others, I am recovering from the influence of the ideals of the world by receiving an infusion of daily connection with our Lord. Such transformation comes from the renewing of my mind[4], because changing my thinking changes my behavior, which then transforms who I am.

To change my thinking, I started delving into the Word of God to understand His purpose and design of woman. Here are just a few truths:

- Genesis 1:27. Like men, women were created in the image of God.

- Genesis 2:18–24. Women were created to partner with man in work, family, and life.

- Proverbs 31:18–31. Women were created to be noble and enterprising.

- Luke 10:38–42. Women were created to learn intimately in relationship with the Lord.

So, once I understood a few basics, I went deep into the Bible and examined women in the Word, to see how they honored the Lord and how He led them. Examples of women throughout the Word give us both positive and

---

[4] Romans 12:2

negative glimpses, leaning into the positives of women like Deborah, Esther, Naomi, Ruth, Abigail, Mary, and more.

I learned that women are savvy negotiators and still nurturers. Women are leaders and world shapers. They often represent a more innocent spirit, and yet women must be astute and discerning. While Jesus was talking to the disciples about what was about to come, He said in Matthew 10:16, "I am sending you out like sheep among wolves. Therefore be as shrewd as snakes and as innocent as doves" (NIV).

We can see this lived out in the life of Esther. She was an orphaned young Israelite woman, living in exile, and raised by her uncle, who found herself in a competition to be the next Queen of the foreign nation. What an amazing plotline!

After Esther became Queen, the King was tricked into declaring an order to allow the slaughter of innocent Israelites throughout his kingdom. It may sound hopeless, but *God had positioned Esther in a place of influence, for such a time as this*[5]. Yet, do not forget the reason there was an opening for a Queen: the King had the previous Queen executed. By the counsel of her uncle, Esther demonstrated excellent communication and negotiation skills while giving respect and honor to her husband, the King. When the King learned that her life was in jeopardy because of his decree, he countered his order by giving the Israelites the power to defend themselves.

---

[5] Esther 4:14

Esther was savvy in negotiating as an Israelite, wife, and Queen. She demonstrated honor to her God by standing up for His people and not compromising His integrity. Her husband was honored when she gently provided him with the information that he did not know when he declared his first decree. Esther demon-

> *She celebrated what God had done and sang praises to Him because God alone was the reason for the victory.*

strated that gentle persuasion carried great strength when led by the Lord. She did this in partnership with her uncle and the Lord.

Judges 4 and 5 tell the story of a great Judge who led her nation Israel through a war that brought peace for forty years. Deborah was a prophetess and wife, called by God to be a judge for a season of restoration for Israel. When the time came to go to battle, she called upon a man to lead, yet he refused to go unless she went with him. In her humble courage, she accepted both Barak's rejection to lead and his commitment to follow her as the "acting General" of the army. When the victory came for Israel against their enemy, she celebrated what God had done and sang praises to Him because God alone was the reason for the victory.

Deborah taught us that humble leaders do what God calls them to do, trusting Him for victory, and giving all honor to Him. She led in partnership with the Lord and the valiant warriors who fought with her.

These are just a couple of examples of godly women from the pages of Scripture. They are real examples that have shaped my thinking and transformed my understanding of what a godly woman of the Word looks like. Leave behind the worldly illusions of lone rangers and the lies that say we can do it on our own. Instead, find strength in our partnerships that are rooted in an intimate relationship with our Heavenly Father. We have nothing to prove because God proved it all through Christ!

Donna L. Clute
www.Coachforpurpose.com

Donna is a wife, mother, and grandmother, trying to live every day for the Lord. She holds a degree in Christian Leadership and Management from Liberty University. She applies that education in her position at New Life Solutions, a life-affirming ministry helping to save babies, save souls, strengthen families, and transform lives all to the glory of God. Recently Donna became a certified Christian life coach and uses this training to help others reach their God-given purpose.

LinkedIn

- www.linkedin.com/in/donna-clute-65ab399

iWork4Him Shows

- http://bit.ly/3q0bqUK
- http://bit.ly/2XnkPJL

Chapter 7 Questions

1. Consider a time when you attempted to "go it alone" just to prove to someone that you aren't a weakling that needs help. How did that work out for you?

2. Donna details a responsibility list based on her life. What order do you currently have your life's responsibility list in: God, Husband, Family, Work?

3. How do you try to prove your worth? How does your behavior affect others?

4. How do you restore relationships injured by your behavior?

5. Esther and Deborah are two courageous examples of women who didn't work alone but worked alongside the Lord to accomplish great things. How is the Lord using you to accomplish His will?

6. What did you hear Donna say?

7. How will this impact your work?

8

Women and Faith: Our Purpose at Work

Ellie Nieves

MANY CHRISTIAN CAREER WOMEN are on a quest for significance. We desire to live our lives and spend our days contributing to the greater good. Finding our purpose is the
driving force for many Christian career women.

I'm a Christ-follower, a wife, a stepmom, a runner, a
road warrior, and a breast cancer survivor. By day, I'm an
attorney in Government Affairs for a Fortune 250 company. By night, I'm a Women's Leadership Speaker and
Coach who is passionate about helping high achieving
women to show up, speak up, and step up in their careers.

I've spent close to 20 years in the workforce, and I
know what it's like to climb up the career ladder—a climb
that comes with many highs and lows. I've dealt with
promotions and job loss, good bosses and bad managers,
collaborative colleagues, and mean co-workers.

When I became a Christian, *I had a hard time aligning my life as a working woman with my faith.*

I didn't speak about my accomplishments because I didn't want to be boastful.

I didn't pursue higher-visibility assignments because I wanted to be humble.

I didn't want to ask for a raise because I didn't want to be greedy.

Ultimately, I believed that seeking a promotion at work would lead to compromising my values.

I once heard that we teach what we need to learn. So, it's no surprise that after I earned my certification in Christian coaching, I focused my practice on helping women develop leadership skills and navigate workplace dynamics.

As I dug into the Bible to help other women, I started to discover God's truth for women in the workplace and how our work relates to our purpose.

The Christian working women I was coaching began to experience breakthroughs as they applied these biblical principles and brought their best selves to work. Many developed better relationships with their bosses and colleagues, others started to get credit for their work, and many earned promotions. And by the way—I did, too!

Advice to help today's working women get ahead in the workplace crops up in the news, in research, and even on social media, but *few voices speak directly to Christian career women.* Therefore, I launched the Christian Career Women Network to equip women of faith in the marketplace with the skills, tools, and scriptural principles needed to navigate the expectations of the workplace as they aspire, achieve, and thrive in their careers and personal lives.

Our Purpose at Work

Many of us may experience a sense of fulfillment in our jobs. We believe that our work is tied to a larger mission. Many of us go to work every day searching for meaning. We want to feel a deeper sense of joy and fulfillment, but we turn up empty. According to *Business Insider*, the average person spends 90,000 hours at work over their lifetime. So, it's no wonder we often believe that what we do for a living must also fulfill our purpose in life. *But our jobs or what we do for a living is not our purpose.*

God designed our work as a way for us to glorify HIM. So, our purpose does not come from the work that we do. Rather, our purpose is manifested in how we go about doing our work. *Our purpose is what we bring to our jobs every day.*

God has blessed each of us with gifts, talents, skills, and abilities. He expects us to put them to work for His glory. A good example in the Bible is the Parable of the Talents. We can find the parable in two places in the Bible: first in Matthew 25:14–30 and again in Luke 19:11–27.

In the Parable of the Talents, a wealthy man is heading out on a trip. Before he leaves, he gives three of his servants money ("talents"). He gives five talents to the first servant, two talents to the second servant, and one talent to the third servant. The first two servants invest the money entrusted to them and double their money, but the third servant buries his talent and does not make a profit. The master is pleased with the first two servants, but he is angered by the third servant. Similarly, God is not pleased when He blesses us with gifts, talents, skills, and abilities that we do not nurture and put to work where He has planted us.

If you work in an environment where your contributions are not recognized, you may feel discouraged or frustrated. You may even stop putting your best foot forward because you believe it's a waste of time. But in Colossians 3:23, the Bible tells us that whatever we do, we should work at it with all our hearts, as though we are working for the Lord and not for humans.

> *Purpose does not come from our jobs— we bring purpose to the work we do.*

As Christian women in the marketplace, we can expect that God will manifest our purpose as we seek to glorify Him every day with our work. The Bible gives us great guidance:

- Commit your work to *Him* (Prov. 16:3).

- Work hard and with enthusiasm (Eph. 6:6).

- Be fair in your business dealings (Prov. 16:11).

- "Do everything without grumbling or arguing" (Phil. 2:14 NIV).

- Help others in need (Acts 20:35).

Remember, rather than looking for meaning and purpose in our work, *we should consider what we bring to our work to make it meaningful and purposeful.* In other words, purpose does not come from our jobs—we bring purpose to the work we do.

Whatever we put our hand to—whether it's at home, church, work, or in our community—God has given us unique talents and skills. Once we identify those talents and skills, it's our responsibility to put them to work wherever we are, *regardless of the environment.*

Ellie Nieves
www.ChristianCareerWomen.com

Ellie is a women's leadership speaker and coach dedicated to helping high-achieving women to show up, speak up, and step up in their careers.

She is the Founder of Christian Career Women Network, a membership organization dedicated to helping Women of Faith aspire, achieve, and thrive in their careers and personal lives.

LinkedIn

- www.linkedin.com/in/ellienieves/

iWork4Him Shows

- http://bit.ly/3hZrnYD
- http://bit.ly/38ot1Qz

Chapter 8 Questions

1. Where do you search for significance?

2. How has God used a situation at work to reveal His purpose for you?

3. If you are having a hard time aligning your work with your Christian faith, like Ellie, what are you doing to rectify this?

4. Ellie mentions that we all have a set of gifts, talents, skills, and abilities by God. How does your set point to significance in your work?

5. What do you think about Ellie's statement that "our purpose is what we bring to our jobs every day"?

6. What is your key takeaway from Ellie's story?

7. How will you apply what you learned from this chapter to your work life?

9

Who's in Control Here?

Sue Wilson

IN PROVERBS 3:5, SOLOMON instructs us to "trust in the Lord with all your heart and lean not on your own understanding" (NIV). What a simple and yet profound slice of wisdom. Yet repeatedly, I have found myself in a place where I am fighting God for control of my life and my current circumstances. Surrendering control of my life to the Lord and trusting the Lord completely with **all** areas of my life and every aspect of my day has been a battle for me, and maybe for you too. Control, trust, and submission have been intimate topics of discussion between the Lord and me for many years.

When I find myself in a place of discontentment, discouragement, or disillusionment, it is often because I'm fighting for the reins of my life, striving to do what I believe is best for me versus what God knows to be best for me, and ultimately failing to submit to God's way.

In Proverbs 3:6, Solomon further clarifies that I not only need to trust the Lord, but I also need to acknowledge

God in *all* ways, and He will make my path straight. This means turning over every area of my life to Him. There are many areas of my life in which I readily acknowledge God, but there are still areas where I attempt to pridefully restrict God, overrule God, or ignore Him. It is very natural for me to bring big decisions to the Lord in prayer, such as major personal financial topics, hiring and firing people at work, and turmoil in relationships. I still struggle with asking God to lead me through all of the little details of my day at work, prioritizing my hours in the day, and the words and thoughts I have on any given day.

The Lord has taught me quite a few lessons regarding these topics of control, trust, and submission. He has used the people I work with, my spouse, my children, and my friends to reveal God's character and to uncover the sin in my life. I invite you to join me as I unpack a few things God has shown me in the areas of relinquishing control, trusting Him completely, and willingly submitting to His will for me.

First, *I must remember how and why I was created*. God created each of us *on* purpose with a very specific and eternal plan in mind (Proverbs 16:9, Jerimiah 29:11). I have been made in the very image of God to bring glory to our Heavenly Father. I certainly do not want to purposefully do anything to miss any step on God's path for me. *So, why do I find myself repeatedly in a place where I am playing tug-o-war with God?* Why do I continue to try and do things my way without first seeking God for guidance? Do I think I know better than God about how to navigate through my earthly life? At the core of this struggle is the fact that I am a sinner.

Next, as a sinner, I've learned the *importance of asking for and receiving forgiveness*. When I find myself fighting for control over an area of my life, there is usually an uncon-fessed sin issue I need to address. To completely trust God and allow the Lord to lead me in my work, home, rela-tionships, finances, and physical wellbeing, I have realized that I must first recognize the sin in my life and humbly acknowledge this sin before the Lord, and then ask Him for forgiveness. I know that the Lord loves a truly repent-ant heart (Luke 15:7). I am a broken, imperfect sinner, and God already knows that. I need not be afraid to express my deep, heartfelt sorrow and regret over the sin that is holding me back or taking control of certain areas of my life. I encourage you to *be honest and ask the Lord to show you where you are grasping too tightly to control certain areas of your life.*

Next, I need to *forgive myself and enjoy the freedom that God's grace and forgiveness offer me.* I know that I can be par-ticularly hard on myself, and I have a long memory. At its very core, this is nothing more than excessive self-judgment rooted in pride. Often, I am holding on to a past failure or sin even though the Lord has already forgiven me. Satan wants me to stay paralyzed by my sin so I can-not effectively fulfill my godly purpose (John 10:10). I need to remember not to let Satan win a battle in my heart that has already been won by the Lord! *Take a minute to reflect on any past sin areas that you may need to let go of.*

When I can recognize and confess the sin in my life, I am in a much better position to *trust the Lord with all my heart and submit my whole life to Him.* I must willingly acknowledge His divine power and sovereign authority over me and all areas of my life. I recognize how difficult this is, but it is incredibly freeing when I can do it! God created women with an amazing intellect and a complex set of feelings and emotions. These gifts allow us to accomplish incredible things for the Lord. These same gifts can cause me/us to stumble when we allow our human nature to kick in outside of God's control.

Submission can have a negative meaning for some, but in the context of a relationship with my Lord and Savior, I have come to view submission in a new way. God designed me with a free will. He has given me the freedom to choose to follow Him, choose to honor Him, choose to worship and adore Him. God desires that I would choose Him and subsequently yield to His authority over me and every area of my life. To do that, I must commit my life to Him and give Him control over my will! Not only must I submit to the Lord, but I must also fully trust in the Lord to completely yield my will. Trust has both intellectual and emotional components that are tightly woven together. The Lord instructs us to put our full trust in Him, as seen in Proverbs 3:5 and Joshua 22:5. This means trusting God with our lives, our work, our family, our finances, etc.

Don't be lured by Satan into thinking we know best, or we can do it all by ourselves. Relying on our own intellect or feelings to guide us through life will not lead to the joy and peace-filled life God desires for us, nor will it lead to following God's plan and path for our lives. Psalm 32:8 affirms for us that when we yield to Him and trust Him, *He promises to teach and instruct us in the way we should go.* He will provide us guidance and counsel and keep His eye on us. God is in control!

So, what might it look like in my workplace and my life when I am abiding in Christ and God is in control instead of me?

- I begin the day by thanking the Lord for the day and asking Him to give me eyes to see all the details of my day through His lens.

- I take time to consult with my Heavenly Father throughout the day, as I am more keenly aware of His presence. He enjoys hearing from me, and He wants to be a part of all my thoughts, conversations, and decisions.

- I find myself pausing at times to listen more carefully for his voice of reason, guidance, or clarity.

- When I find a co-worker or situation a bit more challenging, I ask Him to help me see the person or situation filtered through his love.

- As my day draws to a close, I try to find time for a devotional or reading God's Word.

- I also reflect on my day and can see how God helped me navigate it. The Lord will also reveal times when I took control versus relying on Him.

In 1 King 19, the prophet Elijah had just confronted the Israelites about their double-mindedness and worship of idols. Elijah also had all the false prophets of Baal collected and slaughtered. When Queen Jezebel heard of the slaughter of these false prophets, she declared she would have Elijah killed within a day. Elijah feared for his life and fled. Elijah traveled a great distance over forty days and forty nights as instructed by an angel. He ended up on Mount Horeb in a cave. The Lord spoke to Elijah and told him to go out on the mountain in the presence of the Lord, for the Lord was about to pass by. There was a powerful wind, followed by an earthquake, and then a fire. The Lord was not in any of those things. After all of that, there was a gentle whisper. Elijah heard it, covered his face, and went to the entrance of the cave, and it was there that the Lord spoke with him.

Take time to be still and listen for the Lord's instruction because the world is a noisy place. The Lord often whispers into our lives, and we don't want to miss him!

Yield control of your life to God daily.

Yield control of your life to God daily. Submit each day to the Lord for His will to be done. Trust God with every detail of your day. Watch for God's hand in your day. Celebrate God's goodness and mercy each day. Enjoy His presence!

Verses from God's Word

Submit yourselves, then, to God. Resist the devil, and he will flee from you. Come near to God and He will come near to you … Humble yourselves before the Lord … (Jas. 4:7, 8 and 10 NIV)

Trust in the Lord with all your heart [*soul and mind*] and lean *not* on your own understanding; in all your ways acknowledge him, and he will make your path straight. (Prov. 3:5–6, emphasis added)

I will instruct you and teach you in the way which you should go; I will counsel you with my eye upon you. (Ps. 32:8 ESV)

Sue Wilson

Sue is currently the CFO and EVP at Driessen Water, Inc. in Owatonna, MN. Sue has over thirty-five years of financial and operational leadership experience as a CPA in various service organizations and non-profits. Sue has also been an adjunct faculty member at two different faith-based colleges and universities. She has served on several non-profit boards and councils and currently serves on the Board of Directors and is the Treasurer for iWork4Him.

Sue is married to Jeff, and they have two adult children and three grandchildren.

LinkedIn

- www.linkedin.com/in/susan-wilson-cpa-970aaa12/

iWork4Him Shows

- http://bit.ly/2Lfq63A
- http://bit.ly/38ovA59
- http://bit.ly/35hazXN
- http://bit.ly/2MIThN4

Chapter 9 Questions

1. In what area of your life do you find it difficult to trust the Lord? Why? What is holding you back?

2. What is the potential cost or consequences of holding onto control of this part of your life?

3. Do you struggle with the word submission? If yes, explain why.

4. In a few prayerful words, use the space below to ask the Lord to reveal your life areas that you are trying to control.

5. What will it take for you to trust the Lord enough to release control of the area(s) in your life that you are gripping too tightly?

6. List the name of another godly woman that you can ask to hold you accountable for releasing these areas of control to the Lord?

7. What did you really hear Sue say?

8. How is this going to impact your work every day?

10

Making Meaningful Moments Matter at Work

Mollie Yoder

TIME. THAT WAS THE consistent answer from working women across the country when iWork4Him asked what they needed most.

While we beg for more of it, I think our heart cry is to know that we are spending our time well ... that we are doing the most meaningful work in the moments we've been given.

Belle Cooper of the RescueTime blog shares, "A meaningful life is about connecting with and helping others." The way to wring the most meaning out of each moment is to focus on those God has put in that moment with you. When you are with your spouse, you are *with* your spouse. When you are with your kids, you are *with* your kids. When you are with friends, you are *with* friends. And when you are with co-workers, you are truly *with* your co-workers.

So how do we live in the present and focus intention-ally on who God is putting around us in the workplace? Let's look at three steps that move us toward great con-nection and missional living in the marketplace:

1. Pray up! "Pray without ceasing ..." (1 Thess. 5:17)

Nothing of significance can be accomplished apart from prayer.

Lillian Radke, president and CEO of Unic Pro, Inc., who grew her company tenfold in just three years, shared that she begins each day at the office in prayer before she even cracks open her inbox. I love her logic: "Why would I not make time to meet with the One Person who knows everything that is going to happen in the rest of my day *and* has the power to change it?" Jim Brangenberg, the founder of iWork4Him, once shared with me that he be-gins his day by praying from his bed because, in his words, "once your feet hit the floor, who knows?"

Find the approach that works for you in this season of life and then do it. If we are going *to maximize our minutes, we must adopt the discipline of prayer first.*

2. Love hard! "Show deep love for each other, for love covers a multitude of sins." (1 Pet. 4:8 NIV)

There is this cliché that goes people won't care how much you know until they know how much you care. Yes, it is annoying, but it is also so true!

We are to look like Jesus, and as we explore Scripture, one of Jesus's most distinctive traits *was his irrational, un-conditional, irresistible love for others.* Are you known by your co-workers for your irrational, unconditional, irresistible love?

God placed you in your workforce on purpose. Look around and see who you can love hard today. It does not take grand gestures; a smile and a compliment, a quick handwritten note of thanks, or an offer to help tackle a big or unpleasant part of the work at hand are all ways we can show love to our colleagues. Small acts, tailored to the individual, often take little effort but pay big relational dividends.

While working in an office setting with a team of people, I remember applying the principles of the *Five Love Languages* by Gary Chapman to make sure their love tanks were full. Words of Affirmation colleagues received public praise in the morning stand-up, Physical Touch folks got high-fives after nailing the pitch, offers to run to the copier were for my Acts of Service teammate, a cup of their favorite coffee hit the spot for the Gift-lover in my crew, and a five-minute chat at the water-cooler fueled the Quality Time person in my office. If you are not sure where to start, pop back to Step 1 and ask our all-loving God to show you who and how to love today!

3. Speak truth! "Always be prepared to give an answer to everyone who asks you to give the reason for the hope that you have." (1 Pet. 3:15 NIV)

By the time we have put Steps 1 and 2 into practice, we ought to look very different than the average American worker. So now it is time to take the critical step of speaking truth. Before you cringe and dismiss this as a judgmental, politically incorrect action, rest assured there is a simple, repeatable way for you to share Jesus in His own words—without arguing or passing judgment!

The Pocket Testament League has taught millions of Christ-followers to share their faith more than 150 million times using the Gospels of John. The conversation might go like this: "Susan, thank you for sharing with me about what you are going through with your son. I wanted to give you this; it's the Gospel of John from the Bible, and it has helped me navigate some really difficult times in my own life. I hope you'll read it." Or like this: "Bob, I so appreciated your help on that presentation last week. I wanted to give this to you as a thank you; it's the Gospel of John from the Bible, and it has changed my life." Or even: "Have you ever read any of the words of Jesus? Would you like to?" Then offer the Gospel of John.

It may not increase the moments in your day, but it will certainly maximize the meaning in those moments.

You might even invite a co-worker to read a chapter a day and discuss it over lunch. One group of Christ-followers did this and found they got an 80% "yes" rate from those they asked to do this! However you approach the conversation, *if you are prayed up and have loved them well up to that point, then this next step of sharing the why behind your radical hope and love will feel authentic and not forced.*

We have been given the incredible gift of time—time that allows us to juggle the many roles and responsibilities to which God has called us. Taking the time to be present in each one of those roles—to reflect Christ well to every person God brings our way—takes discipline, but it will deliver eternal results. It may not increase the moments in your day, but it will certainly maximize the meaning in those moments.

Mollie Yoder
www.MollieYoder.com

Mollie Yoder is the Associate Vice President of Marketing and Communications at Trevecca Nazarene University. She is also a wife, mom of two, and reformed rush-o-holic, but most importantly, she is head-over-heels in love with Jesus. Mollie currently serves on the iWork4Him Board of Directors.

LinkedIn

- www.linkedin.com/in/mollie-yoder/

iWork4Him Shows

- http://bit.ly/3nterLI
- http://bit.ly/2L3zM1m
- http://bit.ly/3oopkjm
- http://bit.ly/3pZtezk

Learn more about the simple, repeatable method of sharing Jesus that is mentioned in this chapter by visiting www.PTL.org.

Chapter 10 Questions

1. List the names of three people you work with that you will pray for daily.

2. Do you know your top two love languages? Do you know the love languages of your family (www.5lovelanguages.com) or your team (www.appreciationatwork.com)?

3. If you don't know your family or team's love languages, plan a time to take the tests and discuss them together.

4. Have you shared your faith story with your best "work" friend? Why or why not?

5. Can you think of someone you work with that might be unlovable and how you could show them love? Write their name and an action item.

6. What is your plan to incorporate praying up, loving hard, and speaking truth?

7. What did you really hear Mollie say?

8. How will what Mollie said impact your work?

11

Clothed with Strength and Dignity

Becky Turner

I WAS FINALLY SETTLING into my job as an account executive at a print shop and had just landed one of my biggest sales. I was in my 20's and had just become a follower of Christ. I was shutting down relationships that were unhealthy as well as seeking the Lord more in the Word of God. It was also an exciting time at work.

The order was from a brand-new company that needed everything from logo design to letterhead to business cards to order forms. We were on a tight deadline and were going to make it! That day, I jogged up the stairs to the press room, the smell of ink evident, and the click of the presses sweet. At the top of the stairs stood a six-foot table with stacks of my client's letterhead. Five thousand pieces. I approached them with much joy. The finished product was within reach. But oh, how quickly that changed.

The logo was printed incorrectly! The colors were switched. What was supposed to be light blue was dark blue and vice versa. I was livid! To show my displeasure, I not only yelled at the head pressman, I then swiped all 5,000 sheets onto the floor, stormed out, and headed home for the weekend.

On my hour commute, God got hold of me and soundly rebuked me. "What in the world? A follower of Christ, and you act like that?"

Was I justified in being upset? Of course. But I was not justified in being mean, anger-filled, and vengeful.

Because I'd been intent on getting to know the Lord better, I knew I was wrong and did not argue with Him. I wish I could say instant obedience is always my go-to response. *I repented and then called a mentor and asked, "How can I change?* What can I do to stop responding in the anger I've known all my life and instead respond in peace?"

It was a *long* weekend. I knew I needed to make things right when I got to work Monday morning. Before I could even put my purse down, my boss called me into his office and said, "Becky, I should fire you for what you did Friday. That is not part of our culture nor how we are to act in this office." I wasn't fired. He laid out a correction plan. I was placed in a probationary period. The first step called for me to go upstairs and apologize to the pressmen who cleaned up my mess. *What grace I received from my boss. I never forgot it.*

Over the next months, my co-workers saw a new woman emerge from this train wreck. Through prayer, counsel, and much time in the Word, I truly changed. I was far from perfect, but the short fuse got longer, and the sharp tongue dulled. *The transformation became one of my greatest witnessing tools.*

My life verse is Proverbs 31:25: "She is clothed with strength and dignity; she can laugh at the days to come" (NIV). My entire life, I never had any issues with being clothed with strength. It was the dignity part with which I had troubles. My outbursts (and yes, this was not the only instance—but it was the last) were full of strength but had no dignity.

As I have applied this verse to my life, four key parts have been transformative.

- Clothed
- Strength
- Dignity
- Laughing

First, *clothed*. For me, this meant both clothing the heart and an outward appearance. Yes, God does look at our hearts, but He also says "man looks at the outward appearance" (1 Samuel 16:7 NASB). *If we want to influence the world, we have to accept that our makeup, clothing, body shape, and outside look will impact our ability to reach the world.*

> She is clothed with strength and dignity; she can laugh at the days to come.
> —Proverbs 31:25 NIV

It may seem shallow, but few of us have gotten to the point where someone's outside appearance does not influence us. At least at first. It matters! So, I asked friends about my makeup and used an image consultant. I started exercising and eating healthier and caring more for my body. I also spent more time in the Word seeking wisdom from God because *I believe the more wisdom we gain, the more it will show on the outside.* Proverbs 1:9 and Proverbs 3:22 say that wisdom is an outward adornment. It can be seen with human eyes. So, to be bold in my faith at work, I need to clothe myself well, both internally and externally.

The second part is *strength*. The strength mentioned in this verse is both physical as well as personal or social. As I said, this was not much of a problem for me. I was too strong and needed to tone it down rather than ramp it up. Yet, for many, the ability to both stay strong for the long haul (late night work session or staffing a booth at a trade show) and be confident in our thoughts (defend an employee or champion a business strategy) is challenging. But God did not give us a spirit of timidity but of power and love and self-control (2 Tim. 1:7).

If you are one who needs more strength of the soul—more self-confidence to stand strong—using biblically-based affirmations is the most powerful way to build that muscle. Here are a few affirmations you might want to recite daily:

- I have the right to come boldly before the throne of God to find mercy and grace in time of need (Heb. 4:16).

- I have been given exceedingly great and precious promises by God by which I am a partaker of God's divine nature (2 Pet. 1:4).

- I am firmly rooted in Christ and am now being built up in Him (Col. 2:7).

As we speak truth over ourselves, we renew our minds (Rom. 12:2) and are transformed.

The third part is *dignity*. According to the Blue Letter Bible (www.blueletterbible.org), dignity means to honor and glory and often refers to the splendor of God. It is evident to those around us. How I apply it to my life is respect. First, I respect myself. I do not do things (cuss, lie, gossip, cheat) that disrespect me. It means I believe I am worthy of being treated well. *As a long-time follower of Jesus, the outward show of self-respect is evident. Where I often fail is in the words I speak to myself. Negative self-talk is just as destructive and, in some cases, more destructive.*

Honor or respect does not stop with ourselves but includes others. Albert Einstein said, "I speak to everyone in the same way, whether he is the garbage man or the president of the university." We should treat everyone the same and not think more highly of ourselves than others (Romans 12:3). I remind myself of this character trait in what I call my trash ministry. Whether I am at my church, walking across the parking lot at the mall, or heading into a movie theater, if I see trash, I pick it up. It humbles me physically and mentally. In Christ, the ground is level at the cross.

Lastly, *laughing at the days to come* reflects to those in my workplace that my security, trust, and hope is not in the strategies of man, the stock market, or what the competition does. This joy is rooted in the sovereignty of God.

Regardless of what we do, we demonstrate our faith to those around us. They will see the light or lack of it and can find assurance in the One in Whom we anchor our faith. Our first testimony will always be seen by our co-workers, not heard. First, we demonstrate Christ to the world, and then we can use words.

Resources

- Shari Braendel, Image Consultant
- Jill Swanson, Image Consultant
- First Place for Health, Wellness Ministry
- Becky Turner, Coaching
- Becky Turner's Purposeful Life Plan

Becky Turner
www.BeckyTurner.com

Before Christ, Becky Turner had made a complete mess of her life—relationally, financially, and, especially, spiritually. In 1992, when she came to the end of herself and cried out to God, He graciously swooped in and lifted her out of the pit of her own making and set her feet on a solid Rock. Becky's personal mission is to see the Kingdom of God advanced through stewardship and discipleship. Along with being the National Managing Partner for The Barnabas Group, Becky runs her own coaching and consultancy practice where she works with individuals and ministries to advance their missions and fulfill God's calling.

Book

- www.beckyturner.com/contact

LinkedIn

- www.linkedin.com/in/turnerbecky/

iWork4Him Show

- http://bit.ly/2JYsKdE

Chapter 11 Questions

1. Have you ever displayed disastrous behavior at work? Recall here if you knew you made a mistake or if someone had to call you out on it.

2. If so, how did you handle asking forgiveness for the wrong you did and the hurt you caused?

3. Paul said to Corinth (2 Cor 5:17) that we are a new creation, the old has gone, and the new has come. How is that displayed in your behavior at work?

4. The Proverbs 31 woman being clothed with strength and dignity: how do you feel about what she said about clothing and appearance?

5. Which do you struggle with more, strength or dignity? What can you do immediately to change that?

6. How are you investing in your spiritual walk to become a new, transformed woman in Christ?

7. What did you really hear Becky say?

8. How will this impact your work?

12

Women Workers

Theology of Work Project

FROM TIME IMMEMORIAL, men and women have worked together in whatever enterprise they've found themselves in. In the early American colonies, women worked at tasks ranging from attorneys to undertakers, from blacksmiths to gunsmiths, from jailers to shipbuilders, from butchers to loggers. Some historians tell us that women ran ferries and operated sawmills and gristmills. They ground eyeglasses and painted houses. Every kind of work done by men was done, at least occasionally, by women. Wives had a good knowledge of their husbands' work and often took over the business, running it successfully when the husband died.

But with the developing Industrial Revolution in the early 1800s, "men's work" and "women's work" became increasingly separated to the point that the Doctrine of Separate Spheres became firmly entrenched in people's thinking. Men and women were considered so different from each other that there could be no overlap in their skills or occupations. Any thought of men and women working side-by-side was out of the question.

But that was not God's original design. In Genesis 1:26–28, we hear God speaking:

> Then God said, "Let us make humankind in our image, according to our likeness; and let them have dominion over the fish of the sea, and over the birds of the air, and over the cattle, and over all the wild animals of the earth, and over every creeping thing that creeps upon the earth." So God created humankind in his image, in the image of God he created them; male and female he created them.
>
> God blessed them, and God said to them, "Be fruitful and multiply, and fill the earth and subdue it; and have dominion over the fish of the sea and over the birds of the air and over every living thing that moves upon the earth." (NRSV)

Note that God gave both the man and the woman two tasks: to create families (populating the earth) and to subdue the earth, or more accurately, to be stewards or caretakers of God's creation. Often people assume that the first command about the family was given only to the woman while the second command about stewarding the earth was given only to the man. But that misreads the text. God gave both commands to both the man and the woman. This implies that men should have family responsibilities as well as those in the workplace, and women should have responsibilities in the wider world as well as in the home.

It is in turning the page to Genesis 2:18 that we get a clearer picture of that original command. "Then the Lord God said, 'It is not good that the man should be alone; I will make him a helper as his partner'" (NRSV). Earlier in Genesis 2, the man had been placed in a beautiful garden with the assigned task of tilling it and keeping it. In Genesis 2:18, God creates a woman to work alongside the man in the same endeavor.

God Created Woman as an Ezer Kind of Helper (Gen. 2:18)

Many opinions of working women have been shaped by the word in Genesis 2:18, "helper." This word, therefore, merits some greater attention. Was the woman to be merely a helpful assistant to the man? In our day, we use the word "helper" in the sense of a plumber's assistant, handing the boss the right wrench for the job. But that is far from the meaning of the Hebrew word used to describe the first woman.

> *In Genesis 2:18, God creates a woman to work alongside the man in the same endeavor.*

God created the woman as an *ezer*. The word *ezer* occurs twenty-one times in the Old Testament. In two cases it refers to the first woman, Eve, in Genesis 2. Three times it refers to powerful nations Israel called on for help when besieged. In the sixteen remaining cases, the word refers to God as our help. He is the one who comes alongside us in our helplessness. That's the meaning of *ezer*. Because God is not subordinate to his creatures, any idea that an *ezer*-helper is inferior is untenable. In his book *Man and*

Woman: One in Christ, Philip Payne puts it this way: "The noun used here [*ezer*] throughout the Old Testament does not suggest 'helper' as in 'servant,' but help, savior, rescuer, protector as in 'God is our help.' In no other occurrence in the Old Testament does this refer to an inferior, but always to a superior or an equal ... 'help' expresses that the woman is a help/strength who rescues or saves man."

While many devout Christians see a woman's function as a subordinate to a man, the word *ezer* in the original Hebrew overturns that idea. The woman was not created to serve the man, but to serve *with* the man. Without the woman, the man was only half the story. She was not an afterthought or an optional adjunct to an independent, self-sufficient man. God said in Genesis 2:18 that without her, the man's condition was "not good." God's intention in creating the woman for the man was for the two to be partners in the many tasks involved in stewarding God's creation.

This is an excerpt from a longer article on Women Workers in the Old Testament by Alice Matthews, published by Theology of Work Project. You can find the whole article at www.theologyofwork.org/key-topics/women-and-work-in-the-old-testament.

There is also a companion article on Women Workers in the New Testament at www.theologyofwork.org/key-topics/women-workers-in-the-new-testament.

Theology of Work Project provides resources that help you connect the Bible to your work. You can access this material for free at www.theologyofwork.org. The Theology of Work Bible Commentary is the only commentary covering what the entire Bible says about work.

Theology of Work Project

- www.theologyofwork.org

iWork4Him Show

- http://bit.ly/2LscTo7

Chapter 12 Questions

1. When did you realize that the perspective of a woman staying at home and a man going off to work was a relatively new one?

2. When God created Eve out of Adam's rib, he took Eve out of Adam. Without Eve, Adam was incomplete—only half of the picture, only half of the God-image. How does that change your perspective on your value in society, at home, and within the Body of Christ?

3. What were the two tasks God gave in the garden? What are you doing to accomplish these tasks?

4. What is an Ezer?

5. In the context of God, what is His role as Ezer?

6. What is your role as Ezer? At work? At home? In your community?

7. When you read this excerpt, what did you hear God saying to you?

8. How will this impact your work?

13

Together

Cassy Vos and Cara Willems

WE MET WHEN WE were just 17 and 19 years old. Cassy and her husband, Chad, had already been together for many years, and Cara and Tim had just started dating. We had an immediate connection and became friends quickly. Over the past 15 years, we have worked through our fair share of struggles ... college years, marriage, pregnancies, children, job changes, master's degrees, and dealing with the personal and professional growing pains that naturally come with age. *For many friends, the test of time is too much to handle, and they drift apart to live their separate lives.* We have been able to work through the tides of life, and although there have been seasons in which we weren't as connected, we have always remained a consistent rock for one another.

Friendship in Our 30s

Both of us work full-time, have three kids under the age of eight, a commute, and a full-time working husband. We have a very low-maintenance friendship, which is probably the main reason we have maintained our friendship for so long. Having busy lives and young children makes it hard to find time for ourselves, let alone friends! Throughout the years, we have given one another a ton of grace, especially when responding to calls and text messages in a reasonable time. We have an easier time staying connected now as our oldest kids are in the same grade at the same school, our youngest kids go to the same daycare, and we attend the same church. We have also gone on short family trips together and make a point to have a mom's night out and sometimes even a full weekend together without kids.

For both of us, we learned that you first must focus on yourself and what God has planned, specifically, for you. You have to analyze your gifts and strengths, and many times, those don't become obvious until you've entered the workforce and real life begins. One of the best things about our friendship is that we are very different people. Cassy has a heart of gold, she is sweet as pie, and she is always thinking of others. She is slow to anger and always gives people the benefit of the doubt. Cara tends to be a little more vocal and direct. She is very passionate and doesn't have a huge issue with conflict. One of our favorite scriptures from Proverbs comes from chapter 27, verse 17: "As iron sharpens iron, so a friend sharpens a friend." These differences in character make us a great match as they force us to look inward and soul search to clarify our unique gifts and strengths.

Cara

I am blessed to currently work for an owner that is a strong Christian and incorporates his faith into the culture. We have continuous conversations about our faith and how we are using our gifts and talents in our work to fulfill God's purpose for our lives. I think that incorporating faith at work can be challenging and is an area many Christians struggle with. We live in a culture of being politically correct all the time and being afraid of offending someone. I'm not the most politically correct person, so I haven't had a huge issue just bringing up my faith in conversations with people I work with. *I'm passionate about planting seeds of faith rather than shoving it down their throats.* I'm sure you can look back at your faith journey and attest to the fact that *your faith didn't come to be from one person forcing it on you.* It happens over time and through many experiences that lead you to Him. That is how we lead others to Christ; we plant seeds. I rely on God to give me the clarity to recognize those opportunities and the courage to say what is in my heart. There are plenty of times when it feels as though I overstepped a boundary, and my message wasn't received well, but more often than not, that person will come back and bring up what I said. They heard it, and it forced them to pause and think. We don't

> *I'm passionate about planting seeds of faith rather than shoving it down their throats.*

always know that what we are doing is making an impact, but our job is to listen to God, put our faith into action, and trust His plan.

Cassy

I work in a much more traditional, large corporation setting where faith and God are not as commonly discussed. For me, a big way I share my faith is more about how I present myself, the way I lead my teams, and how I care for others. I take the time to build relationships and truly invest in the people that I work with and around. I navigate each person or relationship individually to determine their personal faith comfort level and adjust my approach accordingly. One benefit, fairly unique to larger corporations, is the opportunity to participate in various social or networking groups. I have the opportunity to participate in our Interfaith and STAR (Stewardship, Teamwork, Advancement, and Retention of Women) networking groups. Our Interfaith group focuses on celebrating and enriching the understanding of faith within the workplace.

> *I take the time to build relationships and truly invest in the people that I work with and around. I navigate each person or relationship individually to determine their personal faith comfort level and adjust my approach accordingly.*

Our STAR group supports women's advancement and retention by promoting advocacy, mentorship, and providing professional development to our employees. I have been blessed with two impactful platforms within my work organization to build relationships, mentor others, and be mentored while also letting God lead me and use me to serve Him.

Our Advice

First, let's begin with advice from scripture. "Therefore encourage one another and build each other up" (1 Thess. 5:11 NIV).

As women, we've both learned to exude courageous behavior while listening to God's will for our lives. This has empowered us to have an impact on others and make a difference. We have worked hard to be more intentional in our faith, leadership, parenting, and interactions with others.

We look to surround ourselves with great mentors (other moms, leaders, friends, etc.) that help build us and challenge us to be the best Christian women, both personally and professionally. Find women that are a reflection of where you're at in life. If you do not have the support system we are talking about, we challenge you to find it. Pray about it. Invest in you and your relationship with God. We are always looking for new resources to learn and grow. Look to Christian leaders with great podcasts, books, local Bible study groups, networking group opportunities, or even just working to put yourself out there and *allow God to lead you and to place the people in your life that you need.*

Recommended Resources

- Your Move with Andy Stanley Podcast
- RISE Podcast with Rachel Hollis
- Jennie Allen's book *Restless*
- Cara's blog, www.purposefulpassion.org

Cassy Vos
linkedin.com/in/cassy-vos-mba-91878912/

Director of Finance, RSM
Wife of Chad
Mom of Natalie, Ella, and Lewis

Cara Willems
linkedin.com/in/carawillems

Operations Manager, Radius
Wife of Tim
Mom to Ben, Wes and Brooks

iWork4Him Show

http://bit.ly/2XrrFhj

Chapter 13 Questions

1. What can you do to permit yourself to hang with friends occasionally?

2. Do you have a friend who has been through much of life with you that you can count on when life gets tough? Who is it?

3. How do you approach living out your faith in your work?

4. If your work environment is like Cara's, where faith is openly discussed, how do you incorporate your faith into that culture?

5. Cassy gets to know her people and then adjusts her faith conversation appropriately. What does that look like for you in your environment?

6. What does it look like for you to focus on God first? Does your schedule reflect that priority?

7. Do you have a mentor? Who is it, or what steps will you take today to find one?

8. What did you really hear Cassy and Cara say?

9. How will this impact your work?

14

Do You Want to Be the Leader Others Will Follow?

Diane Paddison

I WAS CAUGHT IN A very tough situation. One of our clients at Trammell Crow Company had asked one of our leaders to join with him in sharing a one million dollar overage due to a paperwork mistake, or Trammell Crow Company could take the risk of losing one of our largest clients, for which this person was a major decision-maker.

I was privileged to work for a man of integrity, and our CEO was a man of character, too. I went to both of them, explained the situation, and told them I was going to direct our leader to get the documents correct versus to engage in a fraudulent windfall. They both supported me.

Our leader followed through with doing the "right thing." The client didn't fire us. I look back, and I ask, "Why did I even have to think about this decision?" Thank goodness this was a steppingstone in my leadership journey that turned out well on all accounts.

I have been in leadership roles in many of the companies I've been a part of. Each role came with its own pros and cons, but each was a part of following God's plan for my life. I didn't always feel confident in my roles and would sometimes go to God and ask Him if He was sure He wanted me to be at the helm of a team or project.

When you're doubting your leadership abilities or wondering if leadership is where God is wanting you, here is a list of five traits every effective leader utilizes well:

Cast a Vision Others Want to Follow

When you think of Steve Jobs and Jeff Bezos, you immediately recall the mega brands they've built from the ground up. They are not only impactful leaders; they are impactful visionaries. Good leaders won't just dole out "blind" responsibilities to their team. *They will share the vision of their ultimate end goal and share it so well that their team will feel passionately compelled to help get them there.*

Jesus was masterful at drawing others into His vision for the future. They were able to see the long-lasting benefits of their work with him, and it made them joyful and excited to follow Him. It is my hope every day that I can create this same "vision excitement" for my teammates at 4word.

Be Accountable

Have you ever worked under someone who just gave orders and didn't come down to your level to get their hands dirty? If something went south, this type of leader would usually find someone else to pin the blame on rather than shoulder it themselves. Accountability is the cornerstone of empowerment and personal growth. God's Word speaks to accountability several times. James 5:16: "Therefore confess your sins to each other and pray for each other so that you may be healed. The prayer of a righteous person is powerful and effective" (NIV). Leaders don't just lead your team. Be a part of your team. *Nothing makes team members more invested than seeing that their leader is just like them and is willing to roll their sleeves up and get down to business.*

Cheryl Bachelder, www.cherylbachelder.com, a friend and author of *Dare to Serve*, said this: "Whether you act on it or not, you probably know this deep down in your heart: the only legacy of your life will be how you used your gifts to serve others. The only memories left after you depart this earth will be memories of the lives you gave your heart and soul to."

Go Forward with Passion

In Matthew 21:12, what do you think Jesus was trying to say when He drove the money changers from the temple? He wanted everyone to know how strongly He felt about keeping the temple holy and void of greed. What about Nelson Mandela? Do you think he was passionate? Like having a vision, leaders who exude

Leaders who exude an infectious passion for what they do and dream will always leave a mark on their industry.

an infectious passion for what they do and dream will always leave a mark on their industry. One of my good friends and mentees, Liz Bohannon, took her passion for empowering women in Uganda and created Sseko Designs (www.ssekodesigns.com). This thriving lifestyle brand is equipping women in Uganda to be entrepreneurs and support themselves and their families. You can watch a video of Liz and Sseko's story created for the Global

Leadership Summit in 2017. (www.globalleadership.org/vid eos/leading-yourself/grander-vision-liz-bohannon)

Liz had a mentor through the *4word women mentor program* (4wordwomen.org/4word-mentor-program) whose career in investment banking gave Liz access to CEOs who were able to help her with a new business model, the Sseko Fellows program. These CEOs inspired Liz to move in another direction in 2017. Leaders, don't be afraid to show your passion at work.

Inspire Others

All leaders hope deep down that their work and efforts will lead to leaving a legacy. I can't think of a better way

to be remembered than by inspiring someone on your team to accomplish something great. Angela Ahrendts, former SVP of Retail and On-Line, Apple is someone I have been inspired by ever since I learned of her in 2015. Getting to meet her further inspired me to emulate her leadership style. In the Bible, Jesus empowered women by inspiring them. To whom did He appear first when He rose from the dead? Mary Magdalene and Martha, who then went and spurred the apostles into action. *Whatever you do as a leader, perform with the hope that your actions will result in someone down the road doing something truly great.* You may not see that in your lifetime, but that doesn't mean you shouldn't try to be an inspiration, always.

Exhibit Impeccable Character

This may seem like a no-brainer, but I know of too many leaders who are doing incredible things but are doing so at the expense of morals and guidelines. Jesus always did what was right, never sacrificing His purpose even when tempted with a way out of suffering. There will be many occasions where a "shortcut" is within reach, and as a leader, you may think you will never get caught. Why risk that? What would be more in-spiring to you: a leader who had to fight through opposition and roadblocks before ultimately succeeding, or a leader who found loopholes and stepped on everyone around them to claw their way to the top? *Don't be afraid of struggling. As a leader, struggles are a time for you to grow and be a positive role model.*

My friend, Carla Harris, Vice Chairman, Wealth Management, Senior Client Advisor, Managing Director, Morgan Stanley, talked about leadership in Dallas. Carla spelled out leader, and the "A" of leader stood for being your authentic self. She shared that, for many years, she did not tell others she was a gospel singer. When people asked her what she enjoyed doing, she began to humbly share that she sings at Lincoln Center. Prospective and current clients then remembered her! She learned *a part of character is bringing your authentic self into any situation, even work.*

I have been blessed being up-close with these four women leaders and from afar with Steve Jobs and Jeff Bezos to experience these five traits of great leaders. I hope you will ponder your strengths in these areas and grow with God's guidance.

Diane Paddison
www.4wordwomen.org

Diane is the Founder and Executive Director of 4word, a ministry building a global community of Christian women in the workplace. She has a Harvard MBA, is a former global executive of two Fortune 500 companies and one Fortune 1000 company, and serves as an independent director for two corporate and four not-for-profit boards. Diane is a leading advocate for Christian women in the workplace. Diane and her husband, Chris, have four children and one grandchild and live in Dallas, Texas.

Books

- *Work, Love, Pray* (2011)
- *Be Refreshed: A year of devotions for women in the workplace* (2017)

LinkedIn

- www.linkedin.com/in/dianepaddison/

iWork4Him Shows

- http://bit.ly/3hT9haz
- http://bit.ly/3s3Mcql

Chapter 14 Questions

1. Which one of these five traits of great leaders do you exude?

2. Which one are you working on currently?

3. Which one of these five have you yet even to consider?

4. Do you consider yourself a great leader now or a great leader on the rise?

5. How will those around you benefit from your pursuit of these five traits?

6. As a Christian working woman, which of these five traits impacts your world at work and home?

7. Does a Christian working woman need to compromise any of these traits to get to the top?

15

Called to Work ...
and It's Okay

Dr. Tammie McClafferty

WHAT MAKES YOU PASSIONATE about a specific cause or topic? For most individuals, it comes from personal experience, and it was no different for me. My parents had a drastic spiritual conversion, and I was blessed to be raised on the heels of their transformation. Within that context, I had parents who selected a somewhat legalistic church to attend, initially. They were obedient to follow all of the rules, one of which was the idea that it was more spiritual for a woman to stay at home than to work.

Fast forward several years. I graduated from college, established a successful teaching career, got married, had kids, and assumed that now I needed to stay at home because that is what good Christian women do! Except, *I loved my work! I felt called to teach.* I was making a difference. So, I went to the Lord and had a conversation with Him. I told Him that I wanted to teach. I wanted to be a good mom. I wanted to be a good wife. I wanted it all, and I believed with my whole heart that the God who created the universe could help me do it all with excellence!

This is where my passion to be the best Christian working woman began. Firstly, I had to allow the Lord to help me think differently, to think creatively. To be all that I wanted to be, I knew my life may have to look different than what I had projected or dreamed about originally. Instead of a traditional teaching job, I decided to start a daycare and pre-school. In my mind, this allowed me to continue teaching while being with my children. I was hoping to start a small business that served my kids, get it established, and go back to traditional teaching. God had a bigger plan! Remember, He does, "immeasurable more than all we ask *or imagine.*" I couldn't imagine what He was about to do. The daycare and pre-school were hugely successful, and before we knew it, we had franchised out to four locations, had served thousands of students, and had employed more than fifty employees.

After six years of a highly successful business, my husband and I felt God tug on our hearts to take a Sabbatical (this concept alone could be a whole chapter). This led me to go back to seminary to earn a Master's in Religious Leadership. During seminary, *I was still struggling through the concept of being a Christian business leader and all of the "mom guilt" that came with that decision.* I thought it vital to fully understand what God's Word said about women and work, and therefore, chose to do my final thesis on working women of the Bible. What I uncovered was staggering. There is not one verse or example of women in the Bible who stayed at home. Now, we do not know what Mary and some other women did, as the Bible doesn't speak to that topic regarding some, but of the women that the Bible does speak about, they all had a career. Deborah was a judge. Lydia was a saleswoman. The Proverbs 31 woman considered a field and bought it with her own money from her profitable trade business. There was a group of women who gave to Paul out of "their own earnings." These women worked, and they worked hard. Understanding what God's Word said about working women allowed me to free myself from the guilt that I carried over choosing to have a career, and then it freed me to embrace my calling and focus on ways to honor God through my work.

Eventually, I became so passionate about helping other women understand their role and calling in the workplace that I went back to earn a doctorate in leadership and completed my dissertation on the topic of working women. Specifically, I looked at the churches' impact on this particular demographic. I wanted to know the influence, or lack thereof, that the church had on women and their choices to work or not to work. It was enlightening to see the results. Here are a few of the key components that stood out to me and resonated with me from the study. First was the impact of guilt that working women felt from various streams: the church, their home, their friends, their co-workers, and themselves. Interestingly, *the largest amount of guilt these women endured was from within.* They spent an enormous amount of time and energy making themselves feel bad for their work choices. Second was the lack of response from the church to reach this demographic. The church has worked hard to reach the needs of various other demographics but has put little, targeted, or impactful effort into reaching and helping the working mother. Finally, there was a large sentiment felt by these women that their churches did not possess the ability to recognize a woman's calling and to help or equip her to move into her God-given role.

In this study, the research pointed out the true understanding of what the Bible said about working women. Author S. Munger stated in 2015 that godly female leaders such as Deborah, Priscilla, Phoebe, Junia, Tryphena, Tryphosa, and Persis exhibited their prominence throughout Scripture and early biblical times. Likewise, in 2012, M.Y. MacDonald announced that the Bible never identified a woman primarily as a homemaker. Other authors pointed out that Phoebe, Lydia, Priscilla, and many other women in the Bible traveled, worked, and had influential leadership roles (Blake, Pearson, and Agnew, 2013). The Bible did not identify these women of Scripture by their family relationships or their domestic roles. *Rather, their work was a primary focus of their identity (MacDonald, 2012).*

> The research demonstrated the amazing success that women achieved and the satisfaction that they uncovered when they understood their working or their career as their spiritual calling.

Second, the research identified the benefits to women working outside of the home when Ekinsmyth (2014) found that women who worked outside of the home produced a greater sense of value for their entire being. Research has shown many benefits in pursuing multiple roles of career and motherhood, particularly when women view the roles as spiritual callings, and when support systems are accessible (Oates, Hall, Willingham, and Anderson, 2008).

Also, the research demonstrated the amazing success that women achieved and the satisfaction that they uncovered when they understood their working or their career as their spiritual calling. Dik, Eldridge, Steger, and Duffy (2012) defined a calling as the belief that one is called upon (by the needs of society, by a person's own inner potential, by God, by a Higher Power, etc.) to do a particular kind of work. When I embraced my work as my spiritual calling, it was not only more fulfilling, but it helped me begin to alleviate that guilt that I had placed on myself for so many years. Fully understanding that God had gifted me with certain talents and skills and that my vocation was allowing me to utilize those gifts for His greater good, gave me a sense of freedom that I had never experienced before.

Finally, it was unfortunate, but the research showed that the churches have had an overwhelmingly limited impact on working women and did very little to encourage their calling. Churches have emphasized other demographics, such as children's ministry, youth ministry, men's prayer breakfasts (which meet at 6:00 am due to work constraints), and women's ministries (that meet at 10:00 am and provide childcare). However, this does not benefit a working mom who is not available at those times. There is nothing specific to working women and helping them deal with the uniqueness of women in the workplace and how to effectively balance all of their roles.

The outcomes of this research indicated that the largest group of individuals leaving the evangelical churches are working women. It clearly demonstrated that they feel neglected and misunderstood by the church. It also showed that working women do not have extra time and need resolutions that fit within their already tight schedules. *The number one request from the women who were studied in this research was the Sunday morning pulpit time to be adequately shared and utilized to help Christian working women.* A simple example or message topic which includes working women would be a start. Have you ever heard your pastor teach from the pulpit about Priscilla as the CEO of their tent-making company? It would do wonders for these working women to know that their church supports their spiritual calling and their choice to work.

Eventually, I became a Principal of an elementary school, a Professor of Leadership Development and Religious Studies, a Director of a university, and now the Executive Director of a global organization called Lifework Leadership. This is an organization devoted to helping people utilize their work for a higher calling and to help them make a greater Kingdom impact through their careers. *I am blessed to have watched God work through my struggles and successes, and I continue to watch as He develops me into the working woman that He wants me to be.*

As a godly working woman yourself, I encourage you to:

1. identify your calling (*Quarter-Life Calling* by Paul Sohn, a National Lifework speaker who specialized in identifying your spiritual calling)

2. eliminate guilt surrounding your work choices (John 3:17 MSG: "God didn't go to all

the trouble of sending his Son merely to point an accusing finger, telling the world [you] how bad it was. He came to help, to put the world right again.")

3. utilize your work for greater Kingdom impact (*Business God's Way* by Howard Dayton)

Dr. Tammie McClafferty, Ed.D, MAR, MAT
www.lifeworkfirstcoast.com
www.cupofJob.com

Tammie is the Executive Director of Lifework Leadership First Coast, a 9-month faith-based leadership development program to help professionals bring their work and faith into greater conjunction. Lifework has recently opened its first Community Impact Project, Cup of Jōb, in Jacksonville Beach. Most recently she finished her Doctorate in Organizational Leadership from Grand Canyon University. Tammie has been married since 1995 and has three amazing kids: Baylie, Creed, and Canon.

Book

- *Righteous Peer Pressure: A Guide to True Accountability*

LinkedIn

- https://www.linkedin.com/in/dr-tammie-mcclafferty-ed-d-mar-mat-052b441b/

iWork4Him Shows

- http://bit.ly/3999WRr
- http://bit.ly/3hZtmMz

Chapter 15 Questions

1. Do you feel guilty for loving your work? How can you work through it?

2. How would it impact you to hear a sermon that includes examples related to Christian working women?

3. What have you done to help your local body of Christ minister to the Christian working woman?

4. Did you realize the number of biblical women who were business owners?

5. What is your calling?

6. How can you use your God-given calling and leadership platform to encourage and equip Christian
working women to move past the guilt and live out
the call on their lives, as Tammie does? (It doesn't
mean you all have to get a doctorate! ☺)

7. What did you hear Tammie really say?

8. How does this impact your work?

16

Shackles of
Performance-Based Identity

Stephanie Winslow

I WAS THE COMPANY president of our 35-year-old family business when we decided to sell the remaining division. All was said and done, the sale was complete, and all loose ends were tied up nice and tidy. I walked out of the office for the last time. I walked to my car and opened the door to get in.

I turned on the car and put my hands on the steering wheel to back out of my parking spot for the last time. Then it hit me like the compounding weight of an anchor dropped out to sea. A wave of tears rushed from my eyes as the reality of the sale set in.

My mind was whirling with thoughts; my heart topsy-turvy with emotions as I tried to make sense of all I was feeling and thinking. "Now what? What will I do now?" I said to myself. I was frozen, in my car, in the parking lot. I did not want to leave. I did not want to start over.

Driving away from the parking lot was bigger for me than leaving a job. I was leaving my identity behind. I was leaving behind the confident self that existed in the four walls of the family business who knew exactly how she could contribute and what she was good at. Outside the four walls, I did not seem to matter.

I had been so wrapped up in transitioning the business and making sure the new team had all they needed, I had not made time for my own processing. For what felt like the first time in my life, I did not have a plan, a position, or a place to belong to. In my mind, in one moment, I went from a "somebody" to a "nobody."

My last day was a Friday. A weekend of needed rest awaited me once I grabbed hold of the courage to leave the parking lot. Stepping into rest meant I would have to embrace the fear that gripped my heart. It was a fear of the unknown.

That weekend a cacophony of clanging cymbals pounded in my head. Each question pierced my heart with its dissonant inquiry. "Who am I if I am not the president of the company?" "What will I do?" "Will I ever be this successful again?" "Did I make the right choice?"

The months that followed exposed the depths of my fear of the unknown, my fear of starting over, and my fear of the new "me." I was wrapped up in fear that without a title, position, and salary, I was now:

1. Less important
2. Less impactful
3. Less useful
4. Less needed
5. Less likable.

These fears and lies spiraled through my mind. I believed at my core that my work gave my life meaning, and without it, I was *less than*. I felt like I was on the wrong side of life's equation, floating through this life without purpose.

There I was, thinking I was a girl without a purpose. God had other plans that would lead to open doors and opportunities that my stunted vision could not yet conceive.

It was about this same time we began attending a new church where I encountered a group of women willing to walk into the messy places of my life. These women began to address my fears and lies. One by one, they helped me fill my mind with scripture and what the word says about me and what it says about a human's desperate need for community.

I was a woman in need of a community. Over the years, I worked too much and allowed me to isolate myself from any community, especially the church. My identity had been taken hostage, it had been put in shackles, and I believed every word.

I surrounded myself with a community of women who opened my eyes to see God's truth about my identity. God's purpose for my life unfolded through a community of women who would not let me settle for less than God's best for me.

God had and has a purpose for me, but at the time, I could not see beyond my finite view of who I was and who I thought I was supposed to be. With the encouragement of friends in my court, I began handing over one lie at a time to God, and He replaced my fear with His truth.

When I said, "But God, I am less important now because I am not a business leader." God said, "Behold, I have engraved you on the palms of my hands" (Isa. 49:16 ESV).

When I said, "But God, who will I impact, what can I impact now?" God said, "For I know the plans I have for you, declares the LORD, plans for welfare and not for evil, to give you a future and a hope" (Jer. 29:11 ESV).

His plan ... will be the one with greater impact, greater purpose, and ultimately greater depth of relationship with Him.

When I told God, "But God, I am no longer useful." God said, "For we are his workmanship, created in Christ Jesus for good works, which God prepared beforehand, that we should walk in them." (Eph. 2:10 ESV)

When I cried out to God, "But God, I just don't feel needed anymore." God said, "Before I formed you in the womb I knew you, and before you were born, I consecrated you; I appointed you..." (Jer. 1:5 ESV).

When I said, "God, why would anyone like me? I am nothing now," God said, "But now thus says the LORD, he who created you, O Jacob, he who formed you, O Israel: 'Fear not, for I have redeemed you; I have called you by name, you are mine'" (Isa. 43:1).

Through His word and this community of women, the shackles of my mistaken identity were broken. The lies and fears I allowed to grip my mind and take over my thinking were relinquished.

We can trust and put our confidence in God because He has our best interests in mind. His plan and path may not be the timing or the route we would have chosen, but it will be the one with greater impact, greater purpose, and ultimately greater depth of relationship with Him.

Is your identity shackled to your work, performance, or contribution? Are you fearful of what may happen if you lost your position? Have those fears kept you from stepping into a calling God has placed on your life through a new position or business opportunity?

Is your confidence in your ability and understanding, or are you looking to others for wisdom and guidance? Others may challenge you to make the best choice, not the easy one. It is time to surround yourself with the word of truth to break the chains of performance-based identity.

My prayer for you is that you would start your days by simply asking God to show you what you placed your identity in. Is your identity based on who God says you are? Or is your identity based on who you perceive you are and what your abilities say of you?

My second prayer is that you will seek out and find a group of women who will be in the messy middle with you. Find some women who are further down the road of faith, have struggled with identity, and are willing to speak truth.

In the presence of community and the truth of scripture, the fear-mongering shackles of performance-based identity will be shattered. No longer bound by fear, we can experience the freedom to be useful and to make an impact for God. As we press in, we will be reminded that we are wanted and needed. We will come to understand that we are not just likable but lovable daughters of the most high King.

Resources

- *From the Shop Floor to the Board Room: Wisdom for Everyday Business*
- *The Advantage* by Peter Lencioni
- *Hinds Feet on High Places* by Hannah Hurnard

Stephanie Winslow
www.StephanieWinslow.com
www.blindspotconsultants.com

Stephanie spends her days helping women find their voice and making their dreams become a reality in life and business. In her business, Blind Spot Consultants, she partners with women entrepreneurs to help them build lean processes and strategic plans that will enable them to live their best life. Stephanie is a Christian author, blogger, and speaker. She uses her gifts of writing and speaking to inspire transformation in the lives of those who need hope, healing, and restoration. Stephanie's passion is to awaken the complacent and comfort the wounded. Stephanie Winslow is the proud wife of Marshall and the mother of two girls.

Books

- *Ascent to Hope* (2018)
- *From the Shop Floor to the Boardroom* (2019)

LinkedIn

- www.linkedin.com/in/stephanie-winslow-7aa90241/

iWork4Him Shows

- http://bit.ly/3npgJLU
- http://bit.ly/35fYiTJ

Chapter 16 Questions

1. How do you describe yourself?

2. Is your description based on character or productivity and accomplishments?

3. How does your performance impact how you view yourself?

4. How does fear of failure play into your decision making about your career and life?

5. Who in your life has permission to call you out for living in fear and settling for less than God's best for you?

6. If God has our best interests in mind, why do you think it's hard to trust Him with our identities and purposes?

7. What one truth will you implement into your thinking about who God says you are?

17

A Call to Ministry

Dawn Stanford

THIS YEAR I TURNED FIFTY. This milestone birthday makes me pause to reflect over the past fifty years of my life and ask God how He wants me to use the rest of the days of my life for His glory and good. I've been on a journey with Jesus since I was five years old when I gave my heart to Him. Even at that young age, I knew God was with me, and I talked to Him regularly. At age thirteen, I remember hearing about Lottie Moon, the female missionary to China. *That was the first time in my life that I felt a strong stirring to live a life of ministry.*

Through my teen years, I compartmentalized my faith "doing" ministry things, such as being part of Bible studies and Young Life. It was not, however, evident in all areas of my life that I was a Christian. The summer before my senior year of high school I completely surrendered my whole heart to God's Lordship in my life after a series of "God moments", one of which was hearing Billy Graham preach in Denver, Colorado. At age twenty, I took a college semester off to attend a Discipleship Training School with YWAM for six months. Honestly, I thought that I would go off to be an overseas missionary for the rest of my life. That did not happen. He led me back to finish college and embark on my professional life. Through this, *I realized that living a life abandoned to Christ and following Him all my days included my professional life* whether I was in vocational ministry, the business world, a stay-at-home mom, a waitress, or whatever and wherever He called me to serve.

My life mission is "to share my faith in Jesus with others and equip them to faithfully and joyfully live their God-given calling as a child of God in His Kingdom". Some of that *has* been in vocational ministry, but for nineteen years of my professional life, it was in the business world. I owned my own business for twelve years and worked in the corporate world for seven years. *God showed me that business was a tool of ministry.* I asked the Lord to show me how to minister to the people He brought into my circle of influence. Proverbs 15:30 (NLT) says, "A cheerful look brings joy to the heart; good news makes for good health." It was then that I knew God was calling me to be a *"joy-giver"*, and that *joy* is Jesus! God placed me in the business world as my mission field to bring the joyous Good News of His son Jesus and His Kingdom to others.

In those nineteen years, God opened up so many opportunities to build relationships with people I would not have met at church. God opened my eyes to new things and gave me favor and influence in the professional world, specifically to nurture the spiritual lives of professional women. Sometimes after we conducted business, God would place someone specific on my heart to ask if there was anything I could pray for them. In all my years, no one has ever said "no." At times, there might be a strange look or hesitation, but they were always thankful after the prayer. I then committed to regularly praying for those women and would often write a note of encouragement as a follow-up. Through the years, some of these women have, seemingly out of the blue, asked me to pray for a situation or shared with me something God has done in their lives. One friend, in particular, never felt comfortable praying out loud; since we formed a friendship, she now prays freely.

It was in those years God gave me a heart for the Christian working woman. I met so many women who were overworked and stressed. They did not make time to nurture their relationship with the Lord and cultivate thriving relationships with other believers. Much of this was due to their packed-to-the-brim schedules. In 2009, God laid it on my heart to start a Bible study for professional women. Most women's Bible studies offered at churches were during the weekdays, one morning a week, or possibly in the evenings. For the working woman, these times did not fit their schedules. So I thought to myself, "These women have to eat lunch, right? Why not start a Bible study during their lunch hour?!" I invited five other women to meet in the back room of a local restaurant to share lunch and go through the classic NavPress Bible study called Becoming a Woman of Excellence. *These women were already women of excellence in my book, but now they were growing in their faith becoming women of excellence for God's glory!*

As I grew in my relationships with working women, I discovered that many did not fully enjoy their work. It was my passion to help these women find their God-given calling. In 2014, I earned a life coach certification. People would seek me out for guidance on spiritual and professional life decisions, and I wanted to be equipped to coach and mentor them in the right direction. It has brought me so much joy to encourage people to live their God-given calling and to help them discover and use their gifts for His glory. Also, it opened up opportunities for me to speak and teach, whether that be in our local prison ministry, church retreats, professional groups, etc. I *love* doing this, and I come alive speaking to others about the Good News of Jesus and encouraging them to live their God-given calling in His Kingdom.

As you can see, my life has already gone through many seasons. In each of these, I have found ways to be in ministry, regardless of my occupation. My challenge to you is to ask God to open your eyes to see the opportunities of ministry that are in front of you daily. Then, walk in obedience with confidence in God to faithfully take action in that calling. If you sense a stirring from the Lord calling you into something different,

> *I have found ways to be in ministry, regardless of my occupation.*

have an open heart and mind for Him to move in a way you may have never expected. Always remember that *Jesus* is our focus. He is the one who does the ministering through willing servants. We are the vessels He chooses to use for His Glory.

What about you? As you think about your current rhythm of life, could you:

- Serve as a mentor?

- Seek out an older Christian working woman as a mentor?

- Pray with other Christian co-workers regularly?

- Initiate a lunchtime Bible study (or possibly at a coffee shop before going to work for "early birds")?

- Develop personal and soul practices in your current rhythm of life that deepen and not destroy your relationship with God?

- Cultivate relationships with other believers in the Christian community?

Join me in seeking ministry opportunities wherever God leads your feet every day.

Dawn Stanford

Dawn is a lover of *Jesus*, people, coffee, coconut, and *naps*! Extroverted, joyful, and driven. After nineteen years in the business world, God recently brought Dawn back to vocational ministry as the Community and Women's Pastor at New Heights Church in Fayetteville, AR. Dawn's passion and mission are to equip others to faithfully and joyfully live their God-given calling. Dawn has been married to her Mr. Wonderful Rodney for twenty-six years, and they have two daughters, Rebecca (20) and Rachel (18), two cats, Milo and Pablo. They live in Fayetteville, Arkansas.

LinkedIn

- www.linkedin.com/in/dawn-stanford-2870276b/

iWork4Him Show

- http://bit.ly/2XkKIKj

Chapter 17 Questions

1. In what ways do you feel a call of ministry in your life?

2. Have you ever thought about quitting your job so you could work in ministry? If so, what would that look like?

3. Do you compartmentalize life into a work silo and a ministry silo? In what ways could you integrate those two more?

4. Have you ever considered your work as your ministry, no matter what it is? If so, what does that look like for you?

5. Dawn said that business was a tool of ministry. Where can you find biblical proof of that?

6. Dawn started a study over lunchtime. How could you do something similar in your work schedule, whether that be before work, during lunch, or after?

7. What did you really hear Dawn saying?

8. How will this impact your work?

18

My Corporate World Mission Field

Anne Beiler

WHEN I STARTED AUNTIE Anne's Pretzels, I had no formal education, capital, or business plan. I was not an ideal candidate for starting an international franchise organization.

After taking Auntie Anne's Pretzels around the world and selling it shortly after its eighteenth birthday, I can look back and say with confidence that even without those things, I had everything I needed to get started.

When we focus on what we do have, instead of what we don't, we can do more as God develops and leads us.

I had a lifetime of valuable lessons learned because of my Amish household in Lancaster County, Pennsylvania. What my parents taught me formed my foundation for starting a business.

They taught me to take faith with me wherever I go.

Taking my faith into the office every day was my strength and guide for all the challenges I faced daily. I learned early on that I could influence through my actions more than my words.

They taught me to love and engage with people of all backgrounds. (1 Pet. 4:8)

It became clear to me after managing my first two locations that I was not in the "pretzel" business. *I was in the "people" business.* My heart and eyes were wide open to the needs of the people who became part of the pretzel family. I've always said Auntie Anne's was not about me but rather the company's purpose and the people who built it. By modeling God's love as best I could, *we created a culture of caring, grace, and service.*

They taught me to work hard.

Growing up on an Amish farm, we learned what physical labor meant. From planting and harvesting fields to baking and cooking, we always had more to do. Life on the farm instilled in me that hard work and putting in the extra effort will go a long way.

We built Auntie Anne's on these three principals, and as we grew, God revealed the even bigger purpose He planned for us, which was two-fold:

1. To be *light* in the world of business.

2. To be profitable so that we could *give* generously.

To be light in the world of business. (Matt. 5:13–16)

Auntie Anne's became our ministry. I clearly remember when God spoke to me and revealed that I could be Salt and Light to everyone I encountered. I struggled with this in the beginning because my upbringing taught me that Kingdom work meant being a missionary. As I started the company, I learned the corporate business world was a fantastic place to fulfill the call to "go and tell" and be light to the world.

I learned the corporate business world was a fantastic place to fulfill the call to "go and tell" and be light to the world.

We knew we could influence people in the workplace because our full-time employees were spending more time at work than at church. We had forty hours every week to show God's love and model our faith to our growing team.

The truth is that our employees were our greatest asset, and they are yours too. *There is no better way to live out your faith than to create an environment where you value every employee.*

When we understood this truth, we sacrificed and served our employees in ways that made them feel valued and loved in the same ways God values and loves us. Remember, what your employees experience in your presence is often spoken clearly by what you do, not by what you say.

We started our mission to be Salt and Light with our team first, but eventually, it became our mode of operation in the business community. We even created an acronym out of the word LIGHT and included it in our company purpose statement.

L – Lead by example
I – Invest in employees
G – Give freely
H – Honor God
T – Treat all business contacts with respect

Auntie Anne's started building a reputation within the heartless corporate world of the nineties as a business that valued integrity and is honest and great to work with. I believe this was God's plan all along. He wanted us to understand that we can influence wherever He places us.

To be profitable so that we could give generously.

My greatest joy as we grew the company was that God created Auntie Anne's as a vehicle for missions and giving. Giving became my passion, and for the first time in our lives, we had plenty and were able to give in ways that surprised us!

We not only gave financially, but I quickly discovered many other ways of giving. I could give my time to an employee in need. I could give my faith in meaningful ways. It was as easy as giving plenty of hugs as I interacted with employees, franchisees, and vendors so that people knew I cared for them.

My line became, "We give, to get, to give again." Notice the line starts with giving. *I learned a valuable lesson about giving, which was that you don't wait to give until you have plenty.* Rather than waiting until my P&Ls were profitable, we gave a percentage of gross sales from the very first week in business. As we gave, we received more, and then we gave again. We give, to get, to give again comes from the Bible verse, "Give, and it shall be given unto you" (Luke 6:38 KJV).

Discovering our two-fold purpose is what inspired me to get up every day and be Salt and Light to those around me. *Living out my faith looked different when I became a businesswoman* than when I was a little Amish-Mennonite girl, but God's hand was in all of it.

Growing a company built on faith and integrity required personal growth as well. There were many times the struggle was real, but I knew since God put me in this position, I wanted to be the very best me I possibly could be.

Psalms 32:8 (NIV) says, "I will instruct you and teach you in the way you should go; I will counsel you with my loving eye on you." This verse was God's promise to me that *I could always depend on Him to instruct, teach, and lead me in the right direction.* Because of that, I had a life filled with doing the impossible and astounding rewards.

When we understand who God created us to be, and we live out that understanding, our influence is more significant and more substantial.

Anne Beiler

www.AuntieAnneBeiler.com

Anne Beiler is the founder of Auntie Anne's Pretzels, the world's largest soft-pretzel franchise. After selling the company in 2005, Anne's purpose shifted from pretzels to helping women overcome the pain of their past through sharing their stories.

Books

- *The Secret Lies Within* (2019)
- *Twist of Faith* (2008)
- *Auntie Anne: My Story* (2002)

iWork4Him Shows

- http://bit.ly/398lgxi
- http://bit.ly/3nkKrBz
- http://bit.ly/2Xje8bA

Chapter 18 Questions

1. Anne's encouragement to focus on what we have instead of what we don't have is powerful. Which do you find yourself doing more frequently?

2. What resources, character, skills, or abilities do you currently have to help you develop as a leader?

3. Anne said she was in the "people business." What does she mean by that?

4. Anne saw the corporate business world as a fantastic place to fulfill the great commission. What can you learn from her example that will help you lead with faith?

5. Anne talked more about corporate culture than pretzels. Why is that important?

6. What did you really hear Anne Beiler say?

7. How will this impact your work?

19

Walking by Faith in My Business

Shae Bynes

IN MARCH OF 2012, I experienced that most beautiful "God interruption" that completely changed the trajectory of my life. At the time I was a full-time business owner enjoying growing our family's real estate investing business, coaching aspiring and beginner real estate investors, and running a blog that provided resources to corporate employees who desired to create multiple streams of income.

One of my investor friends contacted me and told me that he met a woman with whom he believed he was supposed to connect me. During the call with her, she told me she believed she needed to introduce me to one of her clients named Antonina Geer. I had my first phone call with Antonina, and it did not take long to realize that there was something divinely orchestrated about our connection.

After getting to know one another for several weeks, I told her that I felt like there was a specific reason why we were connected but was unsure what it was. She sensed the same, so we agreed to pray about it and come back together to discuss it. We discussed some thoughts, but nothing really resonated. We prayed more and came back the following week. Still nothing, but I knew in my heart there was something. We prayed again and came back together a third time, and in that call, Antonina shared that God had given her three words that she wrote down in her journal. She said He gave them to her a while back, but she wasn't sure exactly what the words meant or what she was supposed to do with it. She said the words were "Kingdom Driven Entrepreneur." Immediately after she said it, my spirit leaped and I immediately blurted out, "That's a community. It's a movement, and it starts with a book." For the record, I had no idea what I was talking about. It was a word of knowledge provided in that moment by the Holy Spirit, and it came out of my mouth before I could even think about it or question its accuracy.

We were two entrepreneurs with a heart to please God, so armed with this one revelation and instruction, we put our faith into action. Over the next six months, we sat at the feet of Jesus and inclined our ears to hear what the Father's heart was concerning Kingdom-driven entrepreneurship. We signed an operating agreement for a business, wrote the book, and launched both the book and the movement in November of that year.

Sound unusual and perhaps even radical? It was. We were essentially two strangers from different parts of the country. We met face to face only one time before we signed an operating agreement for the business, and this was only seven months after our initial phone conversation. And while we both had been Christians and business owners for quite some time, neither of us really had been a "Kingdom Driven Entrepreneur" before getting this assignment to start a movement called Kingdom Driven Entrepreneur. We did not arrive on the scene as experts to teach other business owners from our wealth of knowledge and experience. We showed up as two people who loved God and wanted to be faithful and obedient to this assignment despite not being qualified on paper to do it. We took a global community of people along the journey with us and grew individually and collectively in doing business in partnership with God, led and empowered by the Holy Spirit to have a greater Kingdom impact in the marketplace. Many of the steps we took

> *My daily work is worship unto the Lord, ministry (service) unto others, and such a blessing in my life!*

along the way were contrary to the wisdom of men, but we could not deny God's hand and the ongoing confirmation in the details as we took steps in faith.

Intimacy with God was everything for us then, and it is still everything for me today. It is no longer enough to simply do business based on the principles of the Kingdom of God without active engagement with His presence. My daily work is worship unto the Lord, ministry (service) unto others, and such a blessing in my life! Antonina's season in the business ended in 2015, and we are still dear sisters. I thank God that over time He surrounded me with an amazing team for the Kingdom Driven Entrepreneur movement. The past eight years have been the most fulfilling of my life and doing business by the infinite power of God's grace just keeps on getting better.

The moment you accept the invitation from God to do business in partnership *with* Him (rather than just *for* Him), you have truly embarked on the adventure of a lifetime.

> Are you tired? Worn out? Burned out on religion? Come to me. Get away with me and you'll recover your life. I'll show you how to take a real rest. Walk with me and work with me—watch how I do it. Learn the unforced rhythms of grace. I won't lay anything heavy or ill-fitting on you. Keep company with me and you'll learn to live freely and lightly.
> (Matt. 11:28–30 MSG)

Shae Bynes
KingdomDrivenEntrepreneur.com

Shae Bynes is a passionate storyteller, bridge builder, and strategist who ignites and equips leaders to be catalysts for transformation in their spheres of influence. Known as "Chief Fire Igniter," she has reached over a half-million aspiring and current entrepreneurs around the globe through her devotionals, books, courses, short films, and podcasts. Her teaching and mentoring provide inspiration and practical strategies for doing business in partnership with God for greater Kingdom impact in the marketplace. Whether she is sharing on platforms publicly or consulting privately, you can expect Shae to deliver an abundance of truth with love, grace, and contagious joy. Shae lives in the Fort Lauderdale, Florida area with her husband and three daughters.

Books

- *Doing Business God's Way* (2019)
- *Grace over Grind* (2017)
- Many more titles

LinkedIn

- www.linkedin.com/in/shaebynes/

iWork4Him Show

- http://bit.ly/3oughgI

Chapter 19 Questions

1. When your business is going great, would you allow God to interrupt it and send you in a different direction?

2. How would God have to get your attention?

3. Have you ever had a moment when the Spirit of God spoke through you in a conversation where you have no idea where the words came from? How did you respond?

4. Do you have a hard time recognizing God's hand in your words?

5. What does it look like for you to put your faith into action?

6. How can you shift to think of your daily work as worship?

7. What did you really hear Shae say?

8. How will this impact your work?

Appendix A

The iWork4Him
Nation Covenant

ARE YOU READY FOR SOME next steps in your journey? The iWork4Him Nation Covenant on the following page challenges you to look at your workplace as your mission field.

You can join other Christ-followers to make a prayer, care, share, and work commitment. Just download the covenant online at www.iWork4Him.com/jointhenation and join the movement.

The iWork4Him Nation Covenant

My workplace is my mission field, a place of full-time ministry. My workplace ministry manual is my Bible. My calling to my workplace is not a second-class calling. I dedicate my workplace as a mission field for God, and because of Jesus in my life, I am committed to celebrating the work that God gave me.

AS A MEMBER OF THE IWORK4HIM NATION, I COMMIT MYSELF TO:

- PRAYER

    o Pray for my co-workers and/or employees by name each day. (1 Timothy 2:1-5 (NLT) 1 I urge you, first of all, to pray for all people. Ask God to help them; intercede on their behalf, and give thanks for them.

- CARE

    o Find a way to serve my co-workers and/or employees outside of what my job requires me to do. (Galatians 5:13-14 (NLT) 13 For you have been called to live in freedom... use your freedom to serve one another in love. 14 For the whole law can be summed up in this one command: "Love your neighbor as yourself.")

    o Find a way to befriend my co-workers and/or employees outside of the workplace so they will trust me when I share the truth. (Ecclesiastes 4:9-10 (NLT) 9 Two people are better off than one, for they can help each other succeed. 10 If one person falls, the other can reach out and help. But someone who falls alone is in real trouble.)

- SHARE

  - ○ Look for opportunities to pray with people at work when you notice they are having a tough day. (Matthew 18:20 (NLT) 20 For where two or three gather together as my followers, I am there among them.")

  - ○ Be ready to share the hope that is in me, Jesus. (1 Peter 3:15 (NLT) 15 Instead, you must worship Christ as Lord of your life. And if someone asks about your hope as a believer, always be ready to explain it.)

- WORK

  - ○ Work with excellence – be the best and brightest example of a worker in my workplace position. (Colossians 3:23 (NLT) 23 Work willingly at whatever you do, as though you were working for the Lord rather than for people.)

Signature: _____ Date: __/__/__

sheWorks4Him Recommended Resources

ORGANIZATIONS SERVING Christian working women:

1. 4word: *www.4wordwomen.org*

2. Christian Business Women's Connection Tampa Bay: *www.cbwctampabay.com*

3. Christian Women in Business: *www.ChristianWomeninBusiness.com.au*

4. Cubicles & Christ: *www.CubiclesandChrist.com*

5. Grow from your overflow – Deneen TB: *www.DeneenTB.com*

6. Leadership Strategies for Women, LLC: *www.EllieNieves.com*

7. National Association of Christian Women Entrepreneurs: *www.NACWE.org*

8. Pinnacle Forum – women: *www.pinnacleforum.com/women-forums*

9. The Christian Working Woman: *www.ChristianWorkingWoman.org*

10. Unconventional Business Women:
    www.UnconventionalBusiness.org/women

11. Women in Business e-community:
    www.facebook.com/groups/WIBecommunity

12. Women in the Marketplace:
    www.WomeninMarketplace.net

13. Working Women of Faith:
    https://workingwomenoffaith.com

God is starting ministries and groups all over the country for Christians in the workplace. This list highlights women-focused organizations that we have interviewed for iWork4Him and believe they have a lot to offer you. Explore their websites and consider how you can take a step toward growth.

For more Faith and Work resources, go to www.iWork4Him.com or read *iWork4Him,* also available on the same website.

Appendix C

The iWork4Him Trilogy

SHEWORKS4HIM: EMBRACE YOUR Calling as a Christian Woman at Work is part of a trilogy that God has put together. The other two titles are *iWork4Him: Change the Way You Think About Your Faith at Work* and *iRetire4Him: Unlock God's Purpose for Your Retirement.* The following two chapters are the introductions to *iWork4Him* and *iRetire4Him*. These books are a collaborative effort with dozens of contributors specifically focused on giving practical, tactical, factual, and biblical perspectives to the Christian working women, everyday believer, and the Retiree. You will find each of these books has a unique perspective that will continue your journey or help someone you know grow where they are. All three books are available at iWork4Him.com/bookstore.

iWork4Him Introduction

A successful hike into the deep woods requires some useful tools. A seasoned hiker might suggest a compass, a GPS, or specific gear based on the terrain. Veterans even publish booklets to instruct and ensure a better journey. Any way you look at it, you need something to keep you on the right path and headed in the right direction.

Believers need tools and resources for our workplace mission field. We need a guide providing information and how-to's to live out our faith journey in our work. *iWork4Him* is dedicated to that effort.

iWork4Him is a statement of faith. It's a lifestyle that impacts everything we do. It is a permanent paradigm shift in our minds. Being able to say "iWork4Him" demonstrates a deepening of our faith. It is Jesus coming alive in us, in our work.

> Don't copy the behavior and customs of this world, but let God transform you into a new person by changing the way you think. Then you will learn to know God's will for you, which is good and pleasing and perfect.
> (Rom. 12:2 NLT)

So how do we live the iWork4Him lifestyle? How do we stop compartmentalizing our faith while doing our work? How do we apply Romans 12:2 and stop copying the world? We first go to the Bible as our primary resource because it is filled with God's wisdom and examples for living out our faith. We wrote *iWork4Him* as a secondary resource providing the practical, tactical, factual, and biblical resources on how you can live out your faith in your work.

For years, iWork4Him has had a front-row seat to the move of God in the workplaces of Christ-followers in America. We have heard the stories, conducted interviews, and covered the conferences and workshops that focus on this topic. We have gathered these stories and resources in this book to guide us on the path to saying iWork4Him.

You are called to work. It is a gift from God. He created work as a way for us to partner with Him. The workplace is the largest ministry opportunity in the world, and God wants you to join Him there. Let's get ready to go in the field—the mission field of your work. May this journey be life-changing. Permanently.

iRetire4Him Introduction

There is a thread of mentoring stitched through the many phases of my life. In seventh grade, my youth pastor invested time in my life and introduced me to the narrow path paved by Jesus. In high school, a college student mentored me for several years. In my early twenties, two business couples invested their lives into Martha and me, guiding us on the unique path of being an entrepreneurial couple. In my thirties, several pastors devoted time from their busy schedules to help keep me on the narrow road. And in my forties, God blessed me with several mentors to reveal the significance of my work as a ministry. Today I have three men that love the Lord and invest their time to help me to serve God the best way possible.

Mentoring changed my life and can change the trajectory of any life. *It is powerful, it is personal, and it is purposeful.* Jesus used it with His twelve disciples and the seventy-two. Investing your life in that of another is the way to most closely mirror how Jesus spent His time on earth.

I am not retired. I don't know if I will ever officially be retired by the American definition, but living in Florida has allowed me to meet a lot of retirees. Most of my friends, neighbors, and fellow church members are retired. These friends have shared some of their life perspectives with me. They feel like they are off the field and have been placed in the grandstands of life. They feel relegated to watching the youngsters run the plays of life while they sit back and miss all the action.

iRetire4Him is a call to those in the grandstands to come back on the playing field of life, to mentor those running the plays. The opportunity to mentor the next generation is abundant and brings the personal purpose reminiscent of a job well done while allowing the flow of unrestricted faith. *iRetire4Him* is dedicated to helping you find faith-centered purpose in your retirement as you live out the best days of your life. Powerful, personal purpose can be found by investing your life into the life of another in the form of mentoring.

Ted Hains adds impactful stories to the end of each chapter, and you will also meet some great ministries that embrace retirees. Join us on an incredible journey of preparing to live with purpose, investing in others, and joyfully declaring iRetire4Him. I am asking you to spend your retirement years mentoring the next generations. You may be the parental figure referred to in this scripture.

> My son, obey your father's godly instruction
> and follow your mother's life-giving teaching.
> Fill your heart with their advice and let your
> life be shaped by what they've taught you.
> Their wisdom will guide you wherever you go
> and keep you from bringing harm to yourself.

Their instruction will whisper to you at every sunrise and direct you through a brand-new day. (Prov. 6:20–22 TPT)

—JIM BRANGENBERG, iWork4Him

Appendix D

Commit Your Life to Jesus: First Time or Recommitment

I BECAME A FOLLOWER of Jesus at 13, while my youth pastor was mentoring me. I made this decision after seeing that life on my own was headed towards a dead end. Jesus said in John 10:10, "The thief's purpose is to steal and kill and destroy. My purpose is to give them a rich and satisfying life" (NLT). I had seen the thief's work in my life. It left me empty and hopeless. Jesus's plan for my life was the answer I was looking for. I think you will see why.

—**Jim**

The following pages by the Pocket Testament League will help you understand God's ultimate rescue plan for you. This is what changed my life.

If you would like a copy of the Gospel of John, send an email to Jim@iWork4Him.com.

A True Story in Your Hands

The Bible is an eyewitness account of history that has stood the test of time and made a difference to billions of lives around the world.

- Have you ever wondered why you are here on earth?

- Have you ever had a sense that you were made for more?

- Have you ever been amazed by the beauty of this world? Or the wonder of love? While at the same time also being shocked and discouraged by the hatred and evil around us?

There's a Reason You Feel This Way ... You Were Designed for Good

God created the world, and that includes you—and He declared everything He made to be good! In fact, He says you're "very good" because you come from Him!

That longing you have inside yourself for the world to "be right" may seem like an echo—here one moment and gone the next—but don't be confused, that sense of longing comes from God.

Not only do you come from God, but you have purpose. The Bible says that your purpose is to be with God in a world of love and beauty and meaning.

We know that something is wrong—and it is us. It's me and you.

Without God, we choose to live for ourselves. You might think of it as walking away from God.

The Bible calls that SIN. Take a moment and ask yourself, "Do I do things I know are wrong?"

If we are honest with ourselves, we will admit we rebel ... we sin.

When we sin, we break our relationship with God. And everything that was meant for our good gets broken.

Can We Fix This Problem?

Great question! We cannot. Many have tried. Many try to build a bridge to God.

Have you ever tried? Tried to live perfectly? It's impossible, right?

The problem is BIGGER than you may realize. Sin separates us from God forever.

But God Intervened Because He Loves You!

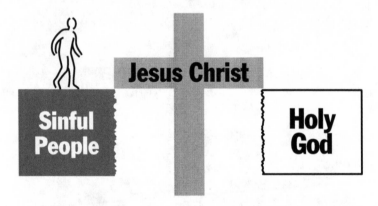

> For God so loved the world that He gave his one and only Son, that whoever believes in Him shall not perish but have eternal life. (John 3:16 NIV)

What you can't do through your own efforts, God the Son, Jesus, did by coming to earth to die on the cross for you. He took the punishment for your sin. Jesus became the way between God the Father and you. Jesus Christ is the only way for us to reach the Father (John 14:6).

What Does All That Mean?

- It means that you can have a real, meaning-ful life—today and forever. "I have come that they may have life, and have it to the full" (John 10:10 NIV).

- It means that when you believe in Jesus, you are restored to the "very good" relationship you were created for... you become God's son or daughter. "Yet to all who did receive him, to those who believed in his name, he gave the right to become children of God" (John 1:12 NIV).

- It means that you can live with passion and purpose because you walk in a loving rela-tionship with the One who created you, serv-ing Him and sharing the Good News of His love with others—reconciling the world to God.

How Can I Know God?

There are three steps to take:

1. Admit that you need God and turn away from sin (see John 8:11).

2. Believe (have faith) that when Jesus died on the cross, He took the punishment for all your sin, and He rose to life again to conquer death (see John 1:29).

3. Receive (ask) Jesus Christ as your Lord and Savior.

A Simple Prayer

Here is a prayer to receive Jesus Christ as your Lord and Savior. It is a suggested prayer. The exact wording doesn't matter, what counts is the attitude of your heart:

> Lord Jesus, thank You for showing me how much I need You. Thank You for dying on the cross for me. I believe that You are who You say You are and that You rose from the dead to conquer sin and death. Please forgive all my failures and sins. Make me clean and help me start fresh with You. I now receive You into my life as my Lord and Savior. Help me to love and serve You with all my heart. Amen.

Jesus said: "Whoever comes to me I will never drive away" (John 6:37 NIV).

What's Next? It Depends

If you prayed the prayer, congratulations. Becoming a follower of Jesus is only the beginning of an exciting adventure. You are invited to read this entire Gospel of John, turn to the back of this booklet, and sign that you've responded to Jesus's call. We've included some additional pages with what to do next and links about where to find resources for the journey ahead.

If you are not ready to respond to Jesus's call, consider reading about Jesus. When people would meet Jesus and ask him questions, his answer was, "Come and see."

So, come and see. You're invited to meet Jesus.

Read the Book of John (if you don't have a Bible, email me for a book of John: jim@iWork4him.com)

The Book of John is an eyewitness account of the life, death, and resurrection of Jesus of Nazareth. John wrote this account with a special theme in mind that he states near the end:

> But these are written that you may believe that Jesus is the Messiah, the Son of God, and that by believing you may have life in his name. (John 20:31 NIV)

My Response

If God has spoken to you and you are ready to follow Jesus, fill out this page as a reminder of your response.

I hear God calling me, and I now know that my sin separates me from Him. Because God loves me, He sent His Son, Jesus Christ, to pay the penalty for my sin by dying on the cross to restore me to fellowship with God. I have asked Jesus to forgive my sins and give me eternal life. It is my desire to love Him and obey His Word.

Name _____

Date of Response _____

Visit www.ptl.org/response and let us know about your life-changing response. We'll send you information about free resources you can use to grow closer to God.

Follow Me

Jesus loves people, and people are curious about Jesus. Jesus's solution is simple. Follow me. For centuries, people have been doing just that: following Jesus.

Becoming a follower of Jesus is only the beginning of an exciting journey. Jesus called it being "born again" (see John 3:3). It means that you now have a personal relationship with God as your heavenly Father. You are not alone. God sent the Holy Spirit from heaven to be your Counselor, to guide you into all truth (see John 14:26; 15:26; and 16:12–15). He will help you live each day for God and to accept the changes He wants to make in your life. You can depend on His power to enable you to grow as a follower of Jesus.

Being a follower of Jesus involves a whole new life. Start now:

- ✓ *Read* a part of the Bible each day.

- ✓ *Pray* daily; talk to God as you would to a close friend.

- ✓ *Worship* God by attending a church where the Bible is taught.

- ✓ *Join* with other followers for support and encouragement.

- ✓ *Share* your faith in Christ by offering people one of these Gospels.

Want to learn more? For a free course on the Gospel of John or to join The Pocket Testament League as a Member (membership is free), visit www.ptl.org/follow.

About the League

The Pocket Testament League is an interdenominational evangelical organization founded in 1893 when a teenage girl and her friends made a commitment to carry pocket-sized New Testaments to share with others. The League encourages followers of Jesus everywhere to Read, Carry and Share God's Word. Learn more about The Pocket Testament League by visiting www.ptl.org/about.

Statement of Faith

The Pocket Testament League adheres to the following statement of faith:

✝ The inspiration and authority of the whole Bible (Old and New Testaments) as the full revelation of God by the Holy Spirit.

✝ The Deity of the Lord Jesus Christ, His virgin birth, His substitutionary atoning death on the cross, His bodily resurrection, and His personal return.

✝ The necessity of the new birth for entering the Kingdom of God, as described in John 3.

✝ The obligation upon all believers to be witnesses of the Lord Jesus Christ and to seek the salvation of others.

Reach the World for Christ! Join the Movement.

If God has spoken to you through His Word, join us today. Go to www.ptl.org/join and click on JOIN NOW. If there is a number in the box below, enter it in the Referral ID field *when you sign up*.

Take the 21-day challenge. Read through the Gospel of John and grow closer to God. Track your progress with your personal dashboard and earn points as you Read, Carry and Share God's Word in the form of pocket-sized testaments. Visit www.ptl.org/marathon to get started!

THE POCKET TESTAMENT LEAGUE®
PO Box 800
Lititz, PA 17543
www.ptl.org

More from iWork4Him

For the retiree in your life

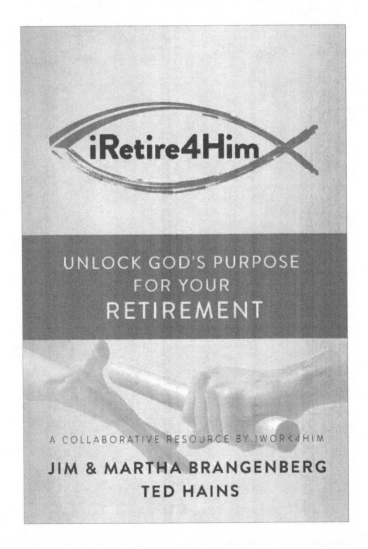